CONSCIOUS EDUCATION

The Bridge to Freedom

Philip S. Gang
Nina Meyerhof Lynn
Dorothy J. Maver

DAGAZ PRESS
ATLANTA 1992

Gang, Philip S., Lynn, Nina Meyerhof, Maver,
Dorothy J.
    Conscious education: the bridge to freedom.

    1. Education   2. Spirituality
    3. Consciousness

Library of Congress Catalog
Card Number: 92-74212

ISBN 0-9623783-2-1

COVER DESIGN AND ART ON PAGE 27   CAROL NEAL-ANDERSON

10 9 8 7 6 5 4 3 2 1

Printed in the United States of America

Printed on Recycled Paper

This book is dedicated to

"Revealing the light in each of us."

In appreciation.

The authors wish to acknowledge the following people who have made a significant contribution to the evolution of this book:

Keith Bailey
Rae Barkley
Caite Bennett
Thomas Berry
Ed Clark
Evie Dorsey
Dorothy & Jim Fadiman
Warren Gang
Elaine Howard
Don Klein
Robert Maver
Ellen McVeigh
Marsha Morgan
Marilyn Mueller
Annie Muller
Robert Müller
Eileen Murphy
Carol Neal-Anderson
Terry O'Keefe
Patty Roeding
Gail Rubin
Margaret Stanicci
Merle Stubbs
Julie Weisberg
Barbara & Dick Wolgamott
Gary Zukav

CONSCIOUS EDUCATION
The Bridge to Freedom

TABLE OF CONTENTS

PART II: FORM

PART III: THE TRANSFORMATION PROCESS

CONSCIOUS EDUCATION

The Bridge to Freedom

Disregarding the superficial chaos which prevents us from seeing clearly, probing beneath the unspeakable disorders that so dismay us, let us try to take the pulse and temperature of the Earth. If we have any power to diagnose we are bound to recognize that the so-called ills which so afflict us are above all growing-pains. What looks no more than a hunger for material well-being is in reality a hunger for higher being: it is the spirit of Mankind suddenly alive with the sense of all that remains to be done if it is to achieve the fulfillment of its powers and possibilities.

Pierre Teilhard de Chardin

INTRODUCTION

We are all connected to all that was and all that will be. On the cosmic scale of time we are but one little link in a great chain of being. Yet in that tiniest of links — a millisecond in time and space — we have changed the course of this planet's destiny like no other life form from time immemorial.

By exploiting *all* its natural resources, we have placed an indelible mark on the Earth's landscape. And, we have endangered its future while witnessing the partial genocide of our own species. Today's issues echo as a cacophony of discordant strands. These disempowering sounds cause individual feelings of helplessness in affecting outcomes, in creating beauty from chaos.

Ours is a world at stress.

In juxtaposition to this tale of degradation is our ever increasing capacity for knowing and understanding, leading us on an evolutionary spiral toward higher order consciousness. It is evident all over the globe. Greater numbers of people are expanding their experience through personal growth, spiritual transformation, meditation, support groups, and metaphysics. These and other lines of personal pursuit are ultimately leading people towards recognizing the universality of humanity. This rising consciousness is based on humanity's potential for cooperation, collaboration, reciprocal altruism and personal and social responsibility.

In our discussions about the future of education we realized our common, unifying strength —we share an interest in the transformation of *consciousness* through education. Further, we have the common vision for a hopeful future rather than a focus on what is wrong with the past and present. With this inspiration, we decided to write together, and share our vision — including the practical steps that we *know* through our collective experience.

What would a system for conscious education look like? What is consciousness? We believe consciousness is a process of expanding personal and universal awareness. This expanding awareness allows people to understand multiple layers of relationships within themselves, to others and in the natural world. What is education? It is the process of "drawing forth" or "leading out" the true Self. We believe that a vision of education can be articulated that embraces the further expansion of consciousness and that the time for this vision is now.

Thus, we began an interconnecting process via phone, fax, telecomputing and mail, from three states, sharing our thoughts, ideas, viewpoints — sometimes struggling to let go of our own individual prejudice — most of the time trusting the process and amazed at our synchronicity. This book is the concretization of our subjective process. We offer it in the spirit of sharing, and hold it out as our contribution to the changing education system world-wide.

We are entering an unprecedented new phase in human evolution. The cultural turning point we are presently experiencing is dramatically shifting our awareness of human limits and possibilities. In conscious education we recognize our interconnectedness and that there is no limit to human potential. Learners are not only given content, but empower themselves through the conscious education process. This process, with spirituality at the core, leads to personal and transpersonal unfoldment. We find this to be true in our own journey, as we each begin to truly experience our own unique place and gift, while creating a whole greater than the sum of our parts.

Our purpose in writing this book is to give educators new organizing principles that lead out from the present day mechanical-reductionist viewpoint towards a more holistic perspective... one that fosters cooperation and peace. It is with gratitude to our triangle, and to the many who have encouraged and supported us in this endeavor that we wish you much enjoyment and an attitude of hope as you join us on this journey.

We offer you this book as an expression of our one-mindedness in the hope that as we share our thoughts, we further the momentum for expanding world consciousness through education.

Dot, Nina & Phil
June, 1992

FOREWORD

EDUCATION and EVOLUTION

There is only one subject matter for education and that is life in all of its manifestations.
Alfred North Whitehead (1929)

AN ANTHROPOLOGICAL PERSPECTIVE

Between seven and ten thousand years ago, two developments in human history occurred that rocked the foundation of our momentum: the accumulation of possessions and the evolution of rigidly male-dominated societies.

A turning point in history took place some 10,000 years ago when hunter-gathering tribes settled in areas where there was an ongoing surplus of food. Once an abundant supply of food became available in a single place, the birth rate increased, the population grew and people began to accumulate possessions. According to Richard Leakey (1978):

> As soon as people depend on anything so discrete as a standing crop, there is advantage to be had in purloining one's neighbor's crops..... Possessions, whether food or other valued materials, invite attempts to gain them by easy means. And as humans can be claimed to be neither inherently evil nor inherently good, but simply opportunistic, it is inevitable that some people will respond to such

> an invitation. And once the successful cycle of
> raiding begins it is very difficult to break. In
> an environment in which a particular form of
> behavior is advantageous, that behavior will
> persist. War is an advantageous pursuit in a
> material world. But it is a product of cultural
> invention, not a fundamental biological instinct.

Today there is a vast chasm between the wealthy nations of the world and those that are marred by poverty, starvation, poor health, economic exploitation and political impotence. Within some of the wealthy nations there are large segments of the population falling into this latter category. Any attempt to re-vision education must take into consideration these inequalities. Could it be that the gulfs that divide nations are political and cultural artifacts and that the true biological nature of humanity is toward cooperation, arising from our common origins and upon which survival is based?

A second turning point in human culture occurred some 8,000 years ago. For thousands upon thousands of years prior to the advent of "civilization," our ancestors lived in an equalitarian society where generative, nurturing and creative powers of nature were given the highest value. Anthropologist Riane Eisler (1987) calls this the *partnership* model of society because both men and women worked cooperatively for the common good. Here, the primary purpose of life was not to compete and conquer, but to cooperate and cultivate the Earth in order to satisfy material and spiritual needs.

According to Eisler, hordes of nomadic tribes from central Asia came west 8,000 years ago causing large-scale destruction and dislocation. These hordes of Indo-European origin brought with them a hierarchic, male-oriented way of life based on warship. Through decimation and bloodshed the partnership model was replaced with the *dominator* model. Women had subordinate roles in the "chain of command." The tools of technology changed from instruments to carry food to instruments of war. These invaders placed a higher value on the power that *takes* rather than *gives* life. They were symbolized by the masculine and ruled by male gods.

So what is humanity's inherent way of being? Dominator or partnership? Eisler's (1987) strong hypothesis is clear:

> In sum, under the new view of cultural evolution, male dominance, male violence, and authoritarianism are not inevitable, eternal givens. And rather than being a "utopian dream," a more peaceful and equalitarian world is a real possibility for our future.

Perhaps these last 10,000 years represent a cultural digression or meaningful evolutionary lesson. Taking human evolutionary time and scaling it down to a 24 hour period, those 10,000 years translate to about three minutes. In this light, during our the first 23 hours, 57 minutes, we followed an innate biological imprint and, only in the last few minutes before midnight, did we embark on this truncated journey.

During these same 8,000 years, humanity has created a pool of knowledge enabling us to explore the deepest chasms of micro and macro existence. We have discovered the unfolding potential of our mind/brain and realized that our destiny is in our own hands. We have created agencies like the United Nations that propagate the notion of a new world order... not an order based on the power of the few, but on the equalitarian views of our ancestors. We have created pathways of greater consciousness that promote independence, free will, self esteem and love. In new and profound ways many people today understand their relationship to the cosmos and their responsibility to themselves and to humanity. There is much to celebrate.

Conventional education quintessentially models the dominator culture. It is characterized by a hierarchical power structure with the learner at the bottom. It is basically left-brain oriented and it facilitates competition and a right/wrong dialectic. It solidifies the status quo by promoting conformity. Emphasis during the last hundred years on measuring output, standardization, mass production and lower cost per "unit" has served its purpose. It is time for a transformation in education.

To transform culture we must reform and liberate the process of education, aligning the rising generation to the *possibilities* of humanity. Radical transformation in the way our culture shares its knowledge with future generations requires a transformation in the *process* of education in order to empower life-long learning.

THE END OF THE CENOZOIC PERIOD

If we could examine humanity in its early stages we would probably discover adults of the species assisting youth in the ways and customs of life. What was at stake was survival and the preservation of the species. We may call it *responsibility*, but it is born in the biological need to sustain our own kind.

Throughout millennia the drive for survival has enabled humanity to persevere. We have been highly successful. We have learned how to manipulate all available resources to serve our needs. This has been accomplished by passing on our instincts, knowledge, morals and values to the rising generations. This transfer-ence of experience is what we call *education*. It has allowed humanity to become the dominant life form during the Cenozoic Period.

As the Cenozoic accelerates towards its demise, what will take its place? Leading evolutionary scholar, Thomas Berry (1990), proclaims that we are on the threshold of the Ecozoic Period.

> The Ecozoic is the emerging period of the integral life community, the fourth in a se-quence of life periods that are generally designated as the Paleozoic (600 - 22 million years ago), the Mesozoic (220 - 65 million years ago), and the Cenozoic (65 million years ago until the present)...
>
> The Cenozoic is definitively terminated. The life systems that were so significant in this period are now so severely damaged that they are no longer capable of continuing their successive waves of creativity. They are all in a state of regression. Our biophysical planet is under assault in its every aspect...
>
> A primary aspect of the Ecozoic Period is that we recognize the larger community of life as our primary referent in terms of reality and value. The earth and the community of species is not a derivative from the human. The human in its every aspect is a derivative from the community of life species; derivative in its being, its functioning, and its fulfillment.

We are the first species on Earth that can consciously alter its existence. We have the knowledge and the vision to transform the planet—for better, or worse. It is the authors' belief that the drive for survival will ultimately overwhelm the thrust of greed and power and that something new will emerge. Part of the "new" is the way in which we transmit knowledge, morals, values and purpose to the rising generation... *conscious education*.

A distinction needs to be made between *schooling* and *education*. The former is instruction that occurs in a specific place or institution; whereas the latter is a process of understanding and awakening throughout life. Schools were born out of the need to deliver the information and skills required for survival in the Cenozoic, as we knew it. They became institutions because the nuclear family, clan, village could no longer keep up with the expansion of knowledge. Specialists known as "teachers" and "instructors" were trained by the ruling hierarchy... the same hierarchy that has led us to the edges of survival.

The whole notion of school demands review and reconstruction as we cultivate the Ecozoic. We must now consider what educational process and form is necessary for human survival. In a sense we need to look at how we transmit our capacity for survival. Is it based on accumulation principles that have dominated the planet during recent centuries? Or, is our future dependent on cooperative, equalitarian models?

How do we plant the seeds for a transformation in education, one that will take us out of the Cenozoic dead end and into the Ecozoic of community and interdependence?

One way is to look at our indigenous past to see if there are certain human attributes or "ways of experiencing" that manifest themselves throughout time. If we can articulate these innately human attributes, then we may gain insight into *natural* education. If we couple this insight with the wisdom we have gathered during this century concerning the path of conscious evolution — the path of love, then education can become a transformed and transformative process. At this point in evolution there is also a growing recognition of humanity's intuitive domain as we are challenged to go beyond the physical, emotional and mental worlds in order to embrace the spiritual.

WAYS OF KNOWING: HUMAN ATTRIBUTES AND LEARNING

According to Mario M. Montessori, son of the famous Italian educator, Maria Montessori, *It is...in studying how (humans) became predominant, one will discover which tendencies enabled that development.* (1956). Montessori goes on to assert that these tendencies or attributes are *"possessed in potentiality at birth,"* and that human beings make use of them to construct their reality and find their way in the world. It follows then, that a positive personal construction will take place if the learning environment is supportive of these attributes.

In looking at our cultural development, what are the basic attributes that were necessary for humankind to predominate? By capturing the essence of these attributes we might begin to see how they manifest in our own lives and how we encourage or discourage their fulfillment in the process of education. We might see how these attributes allow us to follow our genetic and cosmic path. Conscious education looks at these attributes in order to discover what learners bring to unfold their innate purpose.

The educator that takes these attributes into consideration prepares an environment for learners where individuals can fully develop their potential according to natural human evolution. What are these human attributes?

They include; exploration and curiosity, observation, imagination and creativity, intuition, communication and collaboration, responsiveness, and self perfection. There may be others, but these are what we consider essential.

Exploration/Curiosity

A natural tendency is to satisfy curiosity through exploration. In conscious education exploration opens the doorway to experience. Embedded in this attribute is the notion of freedom of choice. This quality in the learning environment implies freedom for learners to satisfy their natural curiosity, to explore and to experience, taking in knowledge through activity.

Observation

The observer is one who is capable of seeing what is happening as a participant in an event. Observation, or visual awareness, is inherent at birth and is a skill that naturally leads to self-knowledge.

Imagination and Creativity

How was the wheel discovered? Where did eating utensils come from? A sense of imaging — imagining abstractly how something might be — is a natural human attribute leading to creativity. Nurturing the creative imagination of every individual is essential to conscious education.

Intuition

Intuition is the extra-conscious part of ourselves, making its presence felt through illumination, understanding, and instant knowing. These glimpses of truth are beyond time (which is a brain event), and are equally independent of feeling. The intuitional realm is beyond the mental and can be reached by way of the imagination. Intuition may well be the most important attribute in conscious education, as it demonstrates that we have answers within ourselves, as well as a means of accessing that knowing.

Communication and Collaboration

In order to *be* with another person, there is a need to communicate, to exchange thoughts and ideas. Thus language in its many forms was invented. Communication implies being with others, leading to community, a natural outgrowth of human evolution. Collaboration or cooperation nourishes the development of community and hence, assures our survival.

Responsiveness

Human beings naturally want to labor for themselves and for the collective whole. In the school setting, an environment based on individual choice fosters a deep sense of personal responsiveness. The conscious educator develops environments in which learners have opportunities to act responsibly. There are four domains of responsiveness: physical, emotional, mental and spiritual. When an individual is responding as a whole person, these domains are integrated. Every domain is valuable and the conscious educator guides the learner to know, appreciate and express each level of response.

Self Perfection

Individuals have an innate desire to fulfill their potential. This led early humans to explore, imagine and create together in order to satisfy their wants and needs. Evolution is a process of self-perfection.

In the following chapters we will explore a new framework for education which includes how these attributes can be nurtured in the learning environment.

PART I
PROCESS

Chapter One

BRIDGE OF CONSCIOUS EDUCATION

Ways of being: Freedom, Independence, Responsibility, Trust and Spirituality

The choice lies in the freedom
of the heart's decision.
To be aware of choice
and to appreciate the freedom
is an act of consciousness
within the knowing potential
of each person...

Katherine Granville (1990)

Conscious education supports the evolutionary process. It is aligned with the Socratic ideal — the nurturing and *knowing drawing out* of the potential within every learner. While it recognizes that content and form are integral to the educational process, conscious education focuses on meaning rather than phenomena. It is a lifelong journey along the bridge to freedom, from a stage of relative unconscious dependent behavior to a conscious responsible recognition of the interconnectedness of all, and individual purpose within that whole.

Utilizing the *bridge* as a symbol gives us a visual picture of the purpose of education. We are, potentially, fully conscious human beings, aware of all levels of our existence — physical, emotional, mental and spiritual. This is necessary

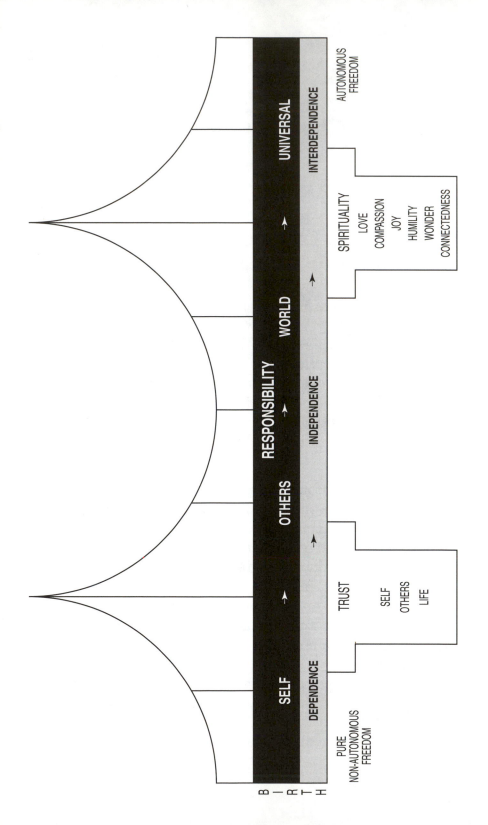

Figure 1.1 Bridge for Conscious Education

for functioning as responsible members of the interconnected human family. However, most of us are not
consciously aware of the whole bridge — rather, we are
only aware of our immediate connectedness to our personal
life and its events. Conscious education creates the environment for knowingly living a life of purpose and meaning in
the context of the whole (Figure 1.1, Bridge for conscious
education).

At birth we enter life's bridge. We are physically separated from our mothers in a state of non-autonomous
freedom. We are still dependent upon others for our survival. As we grow we begin to learn how to take care of
ourselves. We are moving from dependence to independence. During adolescence there is a struggle between the
young person's desire for independence and the parent's
desire for control. When parental control dominates, it
becomes more difficult to secure the level of independence
that is necessary to fulfill individual potential and life purpose.

When personal independence is secured it is possible
to move on towards interdependence. At this stage individuals begin to recognize the existence of an intricate
network of reciprocity, between themselves and others,
between themselves and the natural world, and between
themselves and all of creation.

Responsibility moves through similar successive levels. In our early years we learn to become responsible for
ourselves, to take care of our vital needs. As we grow older
we accept responsibility for ourselves in relation to others.
We develop a sense of service and want to help people we
care about. Personal responsibility continues to expand to
the world or global level. We can see it today as more and
more people are joining together to prevent the further
deterioration of our ecosystem. Universal responsibility

appears toward the end of the bridge. At this stage of human development people understand their deep connection to the web of life and recognize their responsibility to the whole.

At the end of the bridge is autonomous freedom. This holds the space for universal responsibility and interdependence.

What empowers us to cross the bridge triumphantly are the pillars of trust and spirituality. Trust of self is primary. People do not develop self-trust easily unless they are trusted. Thus it is important to invite children to explore, make mistakes, develop naturally and grow to trust themselves. Once trust of self is experienced one can begin to trust others and eventually all of life.

Spirituality manifests as we experience our connectedness. This deep connection to creation evolves over our entire life. It may be experienced as special moments when one is alone in the forest, or when one stares into the heavens on a star-filled night, or observes cloud formations. It is an experience of awe and wonder and an awareness of the oneness of all. Spirituality is the recognition of the inherent beauty, truth and goodness in life. It calls forth such traits as compassion, joy and humility.

One does not teach trust or spirituality. One models these as examples. This is the essence of love.

WAYS OF BEING: FREEDOM, INDEPENDENCE AND RESPONSIBILITY

Freedom is a direct outcome of trusting inner and outer connectedness, and releasing any attachment to form. Freedom of choice is the essential component in safeguarding our evolutionary development. When freedom is honored, independence and interdependence are achieved through responsible action. When one is responsible, one is "able to respond." One cannot respond without a sense of "knowing" and self-confidence which comes through the full unfoldment of the human attributes discussed in the foreword of this book.

Responsible action emphasizes the recognition and acceptance of personal and collective consequences that result from chosen responses. Society can foster the development of responsibility by creating learning environments that stimulate independent choice and by presenting opportunities for inner reflection concerning responsible action.

Societies and communities often set limits for the greater good. One person's *ways of being* should not infringe on someone else's. Individuals may want to drive their car at 90 miles per hour, but doing so would endanger the lives of others — as well as their own. An objective of conscious education is the development of the creative independent thinker who chooses harmless action, in line with what is best for all concerned.

An eight year old who does not like mathematics may want to be free to read every day. The responsible teacher offers the child options through interest and activity. This is a healthy form of limit setting, helping the child develop conscious freedom of choice.

As learners cross the bridge to freedom, they become free, independent, responsible world citizens based on understanding themselves and their place and contribution in the evolutionary process. The conscious educator assists this process by providing a learning environment in which individuals are encouraged to naturally unfold their innate independent selves, knowing that purpose and responsibility go hand in hand.

WAYS OF BEING:
THE PILLARS OF TRUST AND SPIRITUALITY

When trusted, people feel secure and are willing to take risks, explore on their own. Implied in the notion of trust is having respect and confidence in your own as well as someone else's ability to take responsible action. Trusting is giving up control of outcomes. In order to give trust, you have to trust yourself. Trust provides an environment that nourishes and encourages personal growth, open communication and a sensitivity to the environment.

Spirituality is the binding energy of the universe. It manifests itself as our connectedness to everything. It is the essence of conscious education. It frees individuals to experience themselves in relation to all life.

We cannot teach spirituality. It is a state of being. We invoke the spirituality of the learner by our example — living our own truth, honoring all aspects of life as sacred.

This bridge gives further insight on how to create learning experiences that maximize ways of knowing — the innate human attributes that are in potential at birth. It invites us to think in holistic terms concerning the self-directed needs of individuals and groups. It permits us to nurture the human side of development which leads towards conscious evolutionary thought.

CONSCIOUS EVOLUTIONARY THOUGHT

The history of man seems to demonstrate the emergence of his progressively conscious participation in theretofore spontaneous universal evolution... My continuing philosophy is predicated on the assumption that in dynamic counterbalance to the expanding universe of en-

tropically increasing random disorderliness there must be a universal pattern of omnicontracting, convergent, progressive orderliness and that man is the anti-entropic reordering function.
Buckminster Fuller (1963)

The journey towards interdependence and universal responsibility carries with it the notion of conscious evolution. Humanity has now reached a level where it can recognize the meta-processes that are at work in the universe. From the earliest times there have been individuals and groups that have connected with this reality from an intuitive, metaphysical perspective. But today, even the most trusted interpreters of the physical and biological world understand that, beyond the everyday sense of knowing there is a psycho-spiritual connection to the whole.

Interpreters of science like Fritjof Capra (1982), Gary Zukav(1979) and others point to a shift in the scientific paradigm which was characterized by a realization that there is a unitary structure which is reflected at both the micro and macro levels of existence. The Gaia hypothesis is an outgrowth of this viewpoint as it expounds on the notion that the Earth is an integrated living unitary system. Peter Russell (1983), in the *The Global Brain,* has employed both physical and biological perspectives to develop the concept of an evolutionary thrust toward human unity.

Humanity has the possibility of seeing that we are all descendants of the stars and that we are only one part — albeit a very important part — of the story of evolution and consciousness. Conscious evolution then, is the *recognition that I am part of the larger wholeness of life, a great chain of being, and that the well-being of that wholeness is my responsibility too* (McWaters, 1982). This is a central message that must be at the core of the way we educate.

CONSCIOUS EVOLUTION

Conscious education is the pathway of conscious evolution. Consciousness implies awareness, and the ability to observe our thoughts, feelings and actions. *Continuity of consciousness* is a concept throughout philosophical literature. It is described as the ability to remain conscious of where, who and what we are. It implies that we have bodies, emotions and a mind, yet we are not those — we are more than that.

To educate for conscious evolution we need to look at the difference between evolution and involution. The involutionary process takes place when atoms combine to create forms. Involution is a spiraling downward, bringing the subjective life into matter. It has to do with form. Evolution, on the other hand, is a process of gradual perfecting and liberation. It is an upward spiraling, and has to do with the meaning behind or within the form — the essence that creates form. To consciously evolve, to knowingly participate in our own process, and to educate according to the laws of evolution, leads across the bridge to freedom.

Conscious education not only evokes outer form, or phenomena, but also the inner life or true meaning within or behind the form. This has profound implications because it demands that we address the learner from the inner as well as the outer life — as an integral part of the larger whole.

Nature affords the conscious educator numerous opportunities to guide the learner to understand the evolutionary process. When learners study about butterflies — the process of natural evolution from within the cocoon to its beautiful emergence — they see by analogy their own process of conscious emergence from within their own form.

THE SOUL AND CONSCIOUS EVOLUTION

A person's inner life can be referred to as the soul. When we are conscious of our soul connection, and consciously aligned with our innate purpose, we carry with us a sense of self-esteem and a confident attitude.

Some people refer to the soul as the part of us that is the center of feeling and thinking, separate from the body, or as the vital principle, or the breath of life. Others describe the soul as being to the body what vision is to the eye.

The soul is that intangible part of us — our essential Self —the wise part within—the part of us that knows our purpose.

When we speak of conscious evolution, we refer to a life journey based on the knowledge of meaning behind the form. When we speak of conscious *education*, we refer to educating to live life as a soul. In this process we become co-creators in life, and recognize our conscious evolutionary role. Conscious education, based on conscious evolution, is the alignment of meaning and form, soul and personality, evolution and involution, spirit and matter. This leads to natural self-esteem, a true reflection of the inner essence through the outer form.

SELF ESTEEM

Self-esteem is a prerequisite for crossing the bridge towards a life of interdependence and universal responsibility. It is a reflection of individuals accepting themselves. In conscious education self esteem is directly related to one's ability to express one's inner self. Thus self-esteem is the barometer for measuring synchronization with the inner self or soul.

Research has determined (Coopersmith, 1967) that self-esteem may be a more valid indication for success than intelligence. Individuals with high self-esteem generally conclude they are closer to their aspirations than individuals with low self-esteem who regularly set lower goals. This implies that those with higher self-esteem are more in touch with their inner self.

Self-esteem relates to inner and outer bridging, and thus we call it, *conscious* self-esteem. Conscious self-esteem can be enhanced through identification with the personal "I," not through *external* demands and expectations others put on us for behavior, morals, ideals and personal success. Conscious self-esteem reveals itself when individuals express their inner selves to the outer world.

The stages of self-esteem development follow the process of development across the bridge. One moves from self-centeredness to social-centeredness to an interest in the nation, globe and universe. When people feel whole they examine the world and search for their place. As consciousness evolves and the Self is securely in place, a sense of wonderment develops, there is a recognition that all of life is interconnected and a natural desire emerges to actively participate in life.

Chapter Two

DEVELOPMENTAL EDUCATION
and
TRANSFORMATIONAL LEARNING

I never teach my students. I only provide the conditions in which they can learn.
Albert Einstein

Conscious education includes an understanding of developmental processes. These processes have been described throughout this century by leading educators and psychologists. Let us take a look at some existing developmental theories and taxonomies and how they interface with the bridge to freedom.

In biology there is the philosophical concept of *ontogeny recapitulating phylogeny*. Simply stated this means that the life of the individual relives the genetic history of the species. From this biological perspective each human organism incarnates the development of life on Earth — from a single cell through progressive steps until birth. The possibility exists that there is a *psychosocial* development after birth that simulates stages of evolution from an anthropological perspective.

Gang (1989), in *Rethinking Education*, proposes an evolutionary pattern that takes humanity from a state of "in" nature, to "with," "over" and "through" nature. *In nature* refers to the period of prehistory when humans were an intrinsic part of nature and no separation existed between human activity and the natural order. It was a time of unconscious interdependence. *With nature* is the age of agriculture when humanity formed a reciprocal partnership with the natural world through the domestication of plants and animals. During this time science, religion and philosophy were integrated and humanity began to question its relationship to the "outer" nature of things. The last 300 years are referred to as the time of humanity *over nature* because during this period humans, through industrial and technological capability, have sought to dominate and control the natural world. Finally we approach the transition to humanity *through nature* in which humanity embraces nature with the innocence of the epoch of *in nature* and begins to recognize the intrinsic natural order. Humanity through nature is a doorway to conscious evolutionary thought.

It is the prognosis here that humanity does in fact recapitulate the psychosocial development of the species. So it is that the infant lives out an *in nature* behavioral pattern similar to our earliest ancestors; six to twelve year olds experience the *with nature* of early civilizations; and, adolescents, the *over nature* of the renaissance and industrial society. Our challenge today is to help foster the development of the eco-human in the Ecozoic Period — humanity *through nature*.

An understanding of developmental stages sheds light on how and when people learn. If we can derive some general principles concerning the focus of attention during various periods of growth, it may inform our thinking in order to help learners cross the bridge.

Developmental psychology is the study of changes in the patterns of behavior over the span of life. It acknowledges that physical, emotional, social and spiritual development are inextricably linked to chronological growth. Since the 1950's there has been a vast accumulation of research that confirms these processes, offering a developmental context for conscious education.

COGNITIVE DEVELOPMENT

Jean Piaget's classical contribution to psychology was the establishment of stages for logical and cognitive development. Piaget, through a series of intensive experiments, concluded that individuals move through four basic successive motifs of interpretation. From birth to two years was identified as Era I or *sensorimotor* intelligence. The infant toddler interprets the world with the five basic senses through reflex actions. Era II, from two to five years, is characterized by symbolic, intuitive or *prelogical thought*. These first two eras are egocentric in that the locus of meaning is based on the individual's conception of self.

A huge leap forward occurs somewhere around six years of age and continues through the tenth birthday. Piaget called this Era III or *concrete operational thought*. Rules become an essential element for social activity and the child is able to use and manipulate symbols to make meaning out of letters (language) and numbers (mathematics). Another major advance occurs as the child approaches puberty. Era IV is known as formal operational thought. This was Piaget's ultimate cognitive stage of development where individuals are able to think about thinking, grasp simile and metaphor, comprehend abstract concepts of space and time, develop theories, understand proportion and determine cause-effect relationships scientifically.

MORAL DEVELOPMENT

On the heels of Piaget's scheme came the contribution of Lawrence Kohlberg who explains that morality develops in parallel stages. Kohlberg identifies three major eras of moral development, each with two stages. *Preconventional morality* occurs between the ages of four and eleven and is closely aligned with concrete operational thought. Here, the child is basically motivated by fear (stage one) and personal reward (stage two). *Conventional morality* parallels the development of formal operations. During stage three young adolescents make up their minds based on how they believe their parents or peer group would behave or want them to behave. *Good behavior is that which pleases others and is approved by them* (Duska, 1975). During stage four, thinking is based on the dictates of authority. *Right behavior consists of doing one's duty, showing respect for authority and maintaining the given social order for its own sake* (1975). Stage four could very well be the moral limit achieved by most adults.

If conditions are fertile during or after adolescence a transition is made to post conventional or principled autonomous behavior. According to Kohlberg, principled thinking moves beyond dedication to social order and involves *a postulation of principles to which society and self ought to be committed.* Stage five represents a loosening of commitment to the expectations of others and the conventional order and an emphasis on personal standards of social responsibility. The universal ethical principles of stage six are based on a deeply balanced sense of the relationship among human beings and emphasize mutual trust and respect.

DEVELOPMENT AND CONSCIOUSNESS

Consciousness is the totality of a person's thoughts, feelings, awareness and perceptions. As the individual grows from birth to maturity consciousness expands. It may continue along this natural path throughout the life span or it may stagnate if thwarted by psychological limitations. The lowest stages of consciousness are egocentric. Rendor (1989) explains: *Behaviors associated with this level include a preoccupation with self to the exclusion of others.* At the highest levels the boundary between consciousness and self begins to disintegrate and one experiences a connection with the transcendent.

An understanding of how consciousness develops reached a watershed with the work of Kenneth Wilber. Wilber has constructed a "spectrum" of consciousness which begins at birth and follows a developmental pattern akin to the cognitive and moral developmental ladders of Piaget and Kohlberg. However, Wilber's model goes well beyond his predecessors, exploring the highest levels of transcendent being.

The first three "structures" in Wilber's spectrum of consciousness (1986) parallel Piaget's first two eras. The initial structure, *sensoriphysical*, is followed by *phantasmic-emotional*, and *representational mind.* In succession the new-born moves through all three structures—from realms of matter and sensation to mental picturing and finally symbols and concepts.

A major thrust upward occurs as the child moves to the fourth structure, *rule-role mind*, which directly parallels Piaget's concrete operational thinking and Kohlberg's preconventional moral development. Here the child can begin to take the role of others and perform basic mathematical operations. The fifth structure parallels formal operations and conventional moral thinking. Wilber calls this the *formal-reflexive mind* because it is the first structure that is clearly self-reflexive and introspective.

Wilber's sixth structure, *vision logic,* is beyond formal operations and closely follows post conventional moral thinking. He explains (1986): *Such vision or panoramic logic apprehends a mass network of ideas, how they influence each other and interrelate.* A good example of vision logic is an individual's ability to conceive and feel the essence of Gaia.

There are four more structures in Wilber's spectrum: psychic, subtle, causal and ultimate. For our purposes it suffices to say that these are all in the realm of the transpersonal, leading towards transcendence. When we talk about transpersonal experiences we are dealing with consciousness that is beyond the ordinary ego and personality boundaries. They include, but are not confined to, altered states of consciousness, peak experiences, self realization and meditation... all of which "transcend" the traditional, limiting models of human potential.

TRANSFORMATIONAL LEARNING

Let us again look at the model of the bridge (Figure 2.1, Bridge for conscious education with Developmental Taxonomies). Once these developmental stages are superimposed on the structure one begins to see that transformational learning is predicated on the ability of assisting individuals and groups in their movement across the bridge. It is imperative to evolve strategies that aim to draw out the learner's fullest potential at each successive level of development.

Knowledge of these transitory periods can help educators create learning environments that *trans*form rather than *in*form. In-forming is static. It connotes a museum atmosphere, stuffed with information and lacking "engagement."

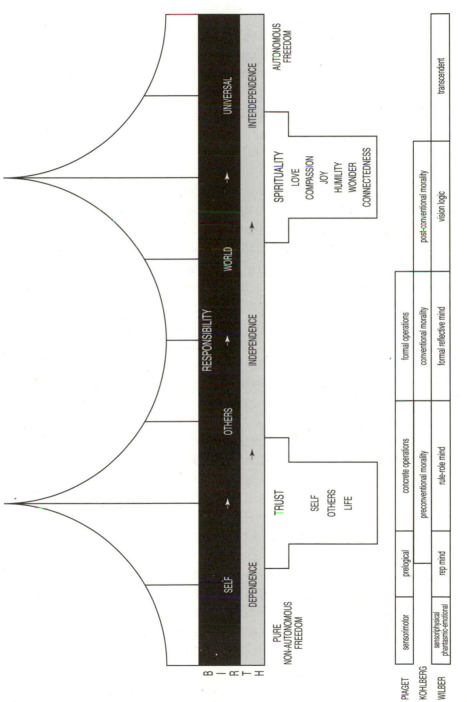

Figure 2.1 Bridge for Conscious Education with Developmental Taxonomies

It might temporarily stimulate thinking, but does not challenge and does not include experience.

Trans-forming experiences produce tension. They leave the learner unsettled in a state of healthy tension, stretching to seek more understanding. There is almost an air of crisis in transformational experience — not the connotation we normally think about. The Chinese word for crisis is **Wei chi**. Wei signifies *warning, dange*r which is our normal reaction to crisis. But Chi means *opportunity for something new to arise*. If we only think of crisis as danger then we are limiting our experience of self.

In a spiritual sense transformation might be experienced through meditation or going inward to explore the depths of one's belief system. A practical example of a transformational experience is the Outward Bound Program. Here an adolescent may be prepared for a rite of passage by being left in the wilderness to survive for several days. The person is trusted to encounter and overcome personal and psychological obstacles. It is through personal experience of body, mind and spirit that the individual transforms.

This suggests that the experiential mode of knowing is a critical element in transformation. In fact, David Kolb (1984) suggests that knowledge is created through the transformation of experience. In Kolb's model all learning begins with a *concrete experience* and, if the right tension is created, moves toward *reflective observation*. Here the learner has an opportunity to think about the experience and to postulate what really occurred. In a healthy learning environment this leads to *abstract conceptualization*. (What does my theoretical framework look like?) Once that framework is designed the learner moves to *active experimentation*. (Does my theory work?) Under certain conditions, a new synthesis may occur resulting in another concrete experience and the process may continue in an upward spiral.

Experiential learning has the capacity to engage individuals at their level of expertise by creating just the right amount of tension to accelerate understanding. It is not limited to childhood education and is fundamental to learning throughout the life cycle.

There is a transformational model for education that has been in practice for over 80 years — predating any theoretical framework for developmental psychology. This model was introduced by Dr. Maria Montessori and continually expanded in scope and depth until her death in 1952.

A TRANSFORMATIONAL MODEL

Before discussing the model created by Maria Montessori, it is important to differentiate the Montessori approach from the movement. The approach, in its purest sense of truth, is an ever unfolding, ever widening conceptualization of how individuals learn. It is based on the innate potential of humanity to seek its own perfection. In reality this truth is within each child. Montessori is known to have said, *"Do not follow me, but follow the child as your guide."* It is the ideas of Montessori that are transformative and can be found throughout progressive education today.

Two years prior to her death, Montessori publicly disclosed her concept known as the *four planes of development*. This model is not the result of a theoretical construct used to measure thinking ability, but a response to 50 years of observation with children as *the* guiding source for understanding. Accordingly, this approach sees the child in full potential, energized by the flame at birth (Figure 2.2, Planes of Development). The horizontal line that connects all of these equilateral triangles is called the line of life. In teleological terms the child is viewed as one whose spirit and intellect are unified, moving towards a "final aim" of self construction and creative potential.

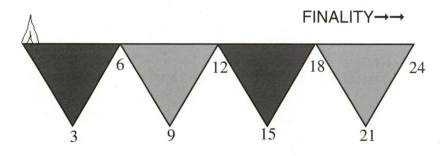

Figure 2.2   The Four Planes of Development

The first and third triangles represent eras of internalization, or as Montessori called them, periods of construction. The second and fourth triangles represent eras of externalization — periods of consolidation. All learning according to Montessori philosophy begins with practical experience. Sometimes this has been misinterpreted in the application of the philosophy by overemphasizing specialized materials as a means to an end rather than a process to observe. Montessori discussed the concept of *materialized abstractions* — materials that are designed to allow the learner to understand complex relationships through manipulation and hand-eye coordination.

The first "plane" is characterized by the *absorbent mind* which takes in all facets of environment and experience without selectivity. The absorbent mind is aided by observable *sensitive periods* between birth and six years of age. Such periods are transitory and heightened times of discovery. Examples include sensitivity to language, order, movement, social relations and sensorial discoveries.

As the child moves through the second plane of development there is an expansion from self construction to identification with peers. Montessori called this identification the "herd" instinct and observed the need to create learning environments for six to twelve year olds that allow for cooperative activity. She noticed how these young people explored the nature of society by creating their own miniature society with its own laws and code of ethics.

When Montessori worked in India during World War II she developed the notion of cosmic education, aimed at children in this second plane. It evolved out of observing the children's awe, respect and sense of wholeness with nature. An approach for presenting cosmic education to young children involves a series of stimulating stories that describe the wonder of the universe and captures the interest and imagination of the child. Imagination, Montessori claimed, is the vehicle for discovery during this second plane of development. It enables the child to go back in time and explore all that was, in order to understand all that is. She urged teachers to sow all the seeds of knowledge through the imagination in order to create lifelong interest in learning.

The secret to accomplish this is to take complex ideas and make them intelligible to the child. In observing an elementary Montessori learning environment one should see children working with huge evolutionary time lines. One might find small groups working with pictures and stories that depict how humans satisfy their needs through time. During this era of concrete operational thought one would also see children developing their own nomenclatures or booklets which describe basic biological, geographical and geometrical features. They create these for themselves in order to grasp a factual reality of how things are organized in the universe.

Like Rousseau, Montessori viewed the period of adolescence as a rebirth or "second" birth. This is the third plane of development when the locus of action moves further away from self and peer group into community and world. Adolescents need a platform on which to try out their newly gained powers of understanding. Unfortunately schools as they are today isolate learners from society rather than integrate them into society.

The last of her four planes may be seen as the final stage prior to being a responsible adult. In looking at Montessori's fourth plane and Kohlberg's post conventional thought it might do well to consider a more open-ended viewpoint. In fact, the bridge itself should not be thought of in terms of a scaled drawing. The length, especially past the midpoint, extends over the entire lifetime of the individual.

Chapter Three

SPIRITUALITY IN EDUCATION

Spiritual attraction is the force that can save humanity. Instead of being merely bound by material interests we need to feel this attraction to each other. These spiritual forces always exist around us. They are the Children! If our soul is far from the child, then we see only his small body, just as we see the star in the sky as a little shining point when it really is an immensity of heat and light.

The art of spiritually approaching the child, from whom we are so far, is a secret that can establish human brotherhood; it is a divine art that will lead to the peace of mankind. The children are so many, they are numberless, they are not one star, they are more like the Milky way, that stream of stars that passes right across the heavens.

Maria Montessori (1939)

Spirituality is the tapestry of existence. It is a thread that unites humanity into one body, one mind and one life. Although as individuals we apparently move independently and often focus on our differences, it is through spirituality that we know the unity in our diversity. In this unity is a deep understanding that, as conscious human beings, we recognize and honor our interconnectedness to all.

Our cultural standards have largely emphasized success through competition, leading to individual achievement. Yet we know the *cooperative spirit* encourages full participation, and leads to group endeavor. What principles will aid in bringing about a practical understanding and a ready application of an educational program whose basis rests firmly and undeniably upon our spiritual reality? Utilizing a holistic framework and the philosophy of education offered by such great teachers as Montessori, Steiner, and Bailey, we address spirituality in education.

When a recognition of oneness and interconnectedness takes its place at the center of a learning environment, it becomes the microcosm of the macrocosm. Learners are recognized as a reflection of the universe — co-creators in their own right. Every human being is innately aware of a unique part to play. Children come into this world as part of the tapestry, weaving and developing a personality which reflects their attributes and experiences. When the soul is honored, and children are encouraged to "be who you are," they develop a sense of self, and tend to become cooperative and self-sufficient world citizens.

Let us now explore the spiritual perspective of the constitution of the human being. This description affords the educator insights into appropriate learning at various developmental stages across the span of the bridge.

SPIRITUAL DEVELOPMENT
(FIGURE 3.1 CONSTITUTION OF THE HUMAN BEING)

- The physical body is our advanced means of functioning in the world. We do not have to think about breathing, digesting, etc., it simply happens. This body is the vehicle through which we experience life. The etheric body is an interpenetrating web of energy which serves as the blueprint for the physical body.

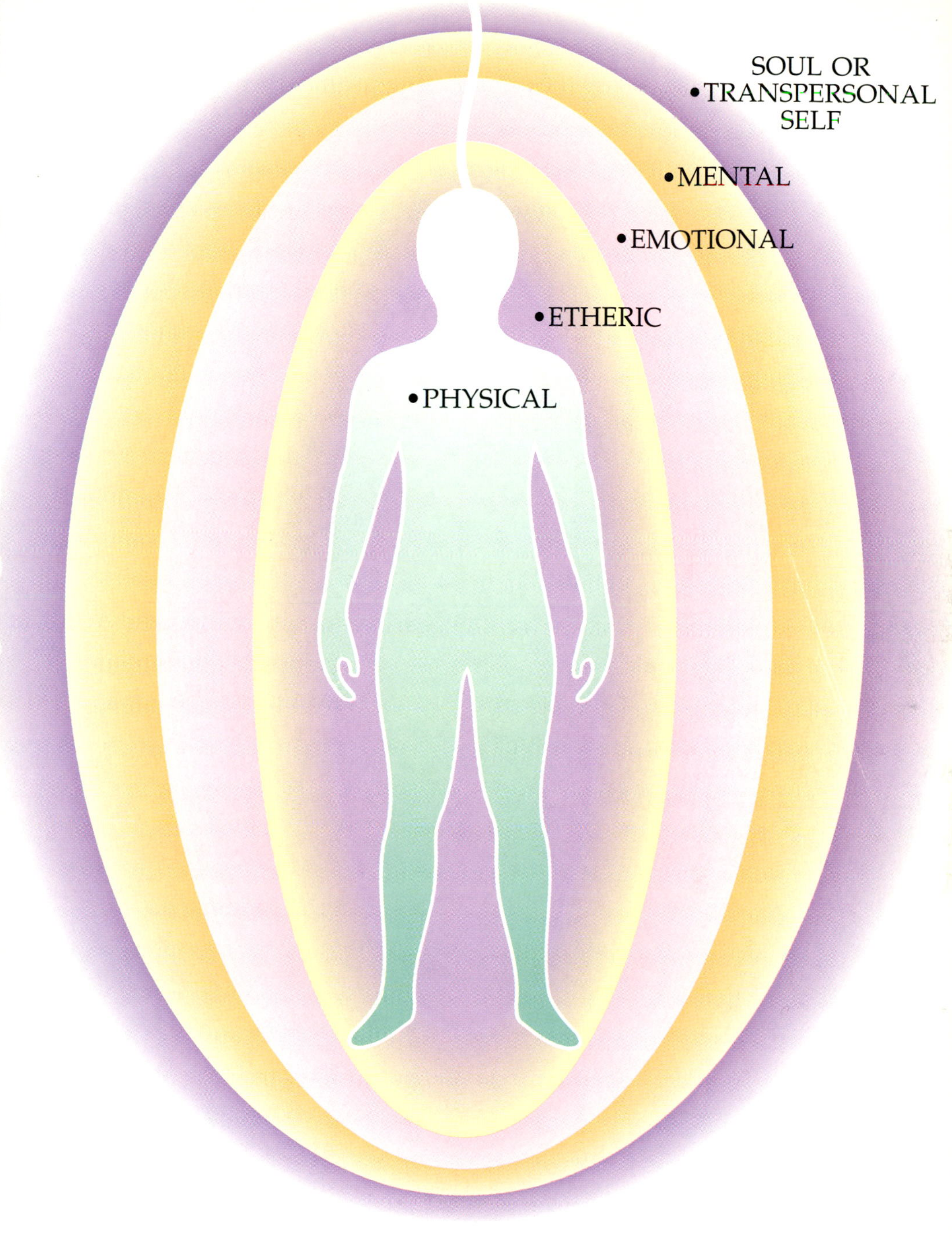

Figure 3.1 Constitution of the Human Being: A symbolic representation of an average human being. The atoms of these bodies are in a constant state of motion and are interpenetrating.

- The emotional body, sometimes referred to as the astral body, is our feeling/desire nature.
- The mental body, or concrete mind, provides us with the capacity to remember, cognate, associate, analyze, organize, deduce and induce, intuit, and create thought-forms.
- The personality is the integration of physical/etheric, emotional and mental bodies, working as a unit of consciousness. In fact, it is not until the physical/etheric, emotional and mental bodies are working together that the personality fully emerges.
- The transpersonal self, or soul, is the seat of our consciousness.

THE SPIRITUAL DEVELOPMENT PROCESS

Developmentally, a human being first explores and learns through the physical body. The second stage of spiritual development includes an awareness of feelings and the nature of desire. The individual learns to self-express emotionally - to emote. As the mental body develops we move beyond being controlled by our emotions and learn to observe and detach from them.

At the next stage the integrated "personality" consciously chooses to experience life through the alignment of the physical, emotional and mental bodies. This is followed by soul infusion. The soul utilizes the personality as its means of expression in the world. This soul infusion leads to self-actualization and expansion of consciousness.

EDUCATING THE WHOLE PERSON

Many psychologists, educators and philosophers, including Assagioli (1983), Kohlberg (1966), Piaget (1950), Wilbur (1986), Saraydarian (1973), Steiner (1965), and others, offer models of developmental stages of human growth and evolution. Let us add another dimension to the developmental learning stages including the spiritual dimension proposed by Alice Bailey (1954) in her book, *Education in the New Age*. (Figure 3.2, Bridge for conscious education with Spiritual Taxonomy)

The first stage of development is *physical*. It includes an etheric component — the blueprint of the physical body — and occurs primarily from birth to age seven. On the bridge this is the first stage, immediately following birth, where there is total dependence, with most individual needs being met by others. During the physical stage of development, it is important to ensure full experience and expression of the senses, as well as the encouragement of the natural curiosity of the child.

The second stage (7-14 years) is *emotional*. While there is still dependence on others, desires are awakening and there is an awareness of something beyond the self. During this time the child consciously experiences feelings, and develops methods for receiving and responding emotionally. Natural development can be restricted if children are not encouraged to learn about and express their emotions during this stage of spiritual development.

The third stage (14-21 years) is *mental*. During this time the individual anchors the necessary tools for creative independent thinking. A sense of independence emerges, and there is the potential of responsible, independent living in the world.

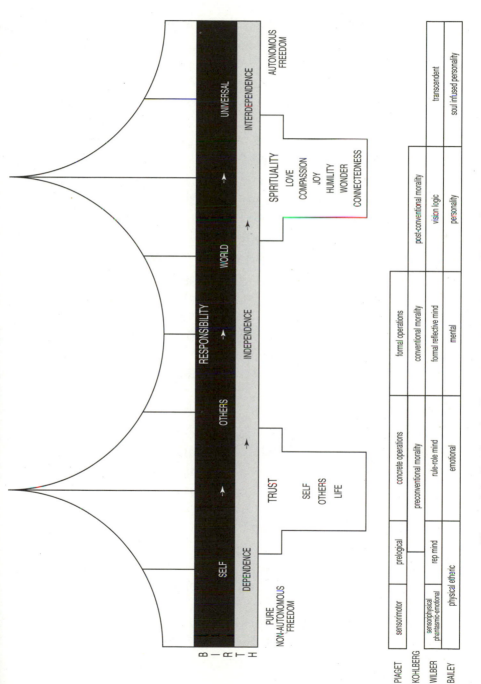

Figure 3.2 Bridge for Conscious Education with Spiritual Taxonomy

Throughout the spiritual developmental scale, these "levels" interpenetrate, and seeds are constantly planted for physical, emotional and mental development. Bailey (1954) suggests that these stages occur in approximate seven year increments beginning at birth, including three year spans of integration and application. Of paramount importance is the nurturing of the creative imagination during spiritual development.

The fourth stage (21-28 years) is the emergence of the *personality*. This level of integration usually yields an independent and responsible individual, and is often perceived when a person steps out into the world and begins to be known by certain traits and skills. However, it can be a limited sense of responsibility, i.e. responsible for self and immediate others. If spiritual seeds are sown during the early years then a more worldly sense of responsibility develops.

The fifth stage (28.....) leading to the ongoing fulfillment of the life purpose as a fully integrated and useful world citizen, is termed the soul-infused personality. This is referred to as a time of getting in touch with your life purpose. During this period, individuals often decide to change careers, or make moves that will more fully satisfy the desire to serve and be a conscious contributor to the well-being of the human family and this planet. The realization of interconnectedness, interdependence and universal responsibility is paramount, and the person chooses to live a more selflessly responsible life.

This is not to suggest that every child follows an exact seven year cycle of learning. It does, however, imply that there is a spiritual developmental process that can help guide the conscious educator. Understanding this process can lead to an education based on natural tendencies and needs, helping children set the stage for realizing their full potential in life.

This spiritual taxonomy implies that when the physical, emotional, mental and spiritual developmental stages are recognized, we, as conscious educators, help give the soul its full expression. During each stage of development there are areas of emphasis that encourage this natural spiritual unfoldment.

We have seen this spiritual perspective applied at the Robert Muller School in Arlington, Texas, USA.

WORLD CORE CURRICULUM

Dr. Robert Muller, former Assistant Secretary–General of the United Nations, and present Chancellor of the University for Peace in Costa Rica, offers a framework for creating a conscious learning environment in his *World Core Curriculum*. Muller refers to each newborn child as a "cosmic unit," replete with its own unique part to play in the universe. How do we create educational environments that empower every child to realize themselves as cosmic units — unique and yet at one with every other unit?

Muller (1982) answers with *The Four Harmonies* in his World core curriculum. He suggests that his curriculum offers a synthesis of all complex knowledge acquired over the last few centuries, with emphasis on the last three decades.*

1) *Our Planetary Home and Place in the Universe* - deals with our planet Earth, and its relation to the universe. Its scope reaches from the infinitely large to the infinitely small, fitting each strand into a clear pattern of interrelationships — the universe, the stars, and outer space to microbiology, genetics, chemistry, and nuclear physics. This body of planetary

---

* This following information is taken from the curriculum guide of The Robert Muller School, 6005 Royaloak Drive, Arlington, Texas, USA.

and universal knowledge can be of value to students of all nations; for out of this understanding can come a knowledge of true world citizenship, based upon a responsibility toward care and restoration of our planet.

2) *The Human Family* - reveals interrelationships of various human groups. It deals with both quantitative and qualitative characteristics of these groupings. As students learn about their human family, they begin to see the beauty of its diversity. They are led to discover the pervading thread of sameness that unites all. Thus is laid a foundation for an understanding which can lead to peace and right human relations among all peoples on our planet.

3) *Our Place in Time* - flows through the other strands of the spiral, giving form to the whole. As humanity sees its relationship to the universe, and its place within that universe, it then must recognize its place in time. The evolving universe is constantly revealing to (humanity) the necessity of responding to the present with the knowledge of the past, while at the same time, maintaining a vision of the future. Students learn through experience that the past is the seed of the present and the future is the flower of possibilities unseen. They learn that action follows thought. They begin to understand how their own actions condition their future. This leads to an understanding of how the interrelationship of national and international events are shaping the future on a larger scale.

4) *The Miracle of Individual Human Life* - presents the four aspects of (humanity): physical, emotional, mental and spiritual. Through the ages, (humanity) has sought for an understanding of the miracle of life. He has searched increasingly for that spark of life which ignites the universe in all its multifarious forms. Science has probed and experimented; religions have sought answers from prophets and sages. From this has come the knowledge that the human kingdom is the most ingenious and creative of all the amazing kingdoms in nature. The knowledge of the human kingdom is the planetary brain, the steward of all the other kingdoms.

A framework such as this might be utilized by educators to develop curricula and create learning environments in line with the spiritual taxonomy for the learner's journey across the bridge.

For example, in *Our Place In Time,* the idea of action following thought leads to the realization of how the learner impacts the world and how the interrelation of national and international events, in turn, shape the future. Young people come to realize the significant part they play in the world.

Introducing concepts at a young age enables people to come into true *knowing* at the appropriate developmental stage. Thus, all across the bridge the conscious educator is sowing seeds for the gradual evolutionary development and understanding of the learner who is, ultimately, the interdependent, universally responsible world citizen.

Chapter Four

PARADIGM SHIFTS AND EDUCATION

We are moving from a culture that emphasizes the study of things in isolation from one another to a culture that emphasizes contexts, relationships and wholes.

Alvin Toffler

During the latter part of the twentieth century, great strides in our understanding of human life in relationship to the natural world have been realized. Yet, perhaps the most significant recent developments lie in the realm of science, which is having a penetrating influence on the changing world view. In the past, science regarded life as a myriad of separate physical manifestations, and an empirical means of categorizing and studying manifestation has been developed. Through the use of technology humans became experts at controlling the external environment. As this century comes to a close we are beginning to recognize the underlying implications of our interconnectedness.

PARADIGM SHIFTS

Fritjof Capra (1982) in *The Turning Point*, offers a new view on the paradigm shifts that have occurred over the last five hundred years. If we look for the roots of our current scientific mainstream culture, we will find them in a dramatic shift in thinking that occurred in the 16th and 17th centuries. Prior to 1500, the scientific framework was based on Aristotle and the Church, as synthesized by Thomas Aquinas in the 13th century, setting the stage for a homeocentric framework.

This outlook changed completely due to the so-called scientific revolution which began with Copernicus' heliocentric view, was reinforced by Kepler's astronomical tables and calculations, and was grounded by Galileo and Francis Bacon. Galileo's empirical approach and use of mathematical models and Bacon's inductive procedure prepared the way for the paradigm shift from an organic view of nature to the metaphor of the world as a machine. This shift was initiated and completed in the 17th century by two towering figures, René Descartes and Isaac Newton.

Descartes believed in the certainty of scientific knowledge. His methods were mathematical and analytic, emphasizing the reduction of complex phenomena to their constituent parts. Further, he insisted on a division between mind and matter, which were presented as independent, separate realms. The universe was a machine, governed by exact mathematical laws capable of objective interpretation.

Newton synthesized the Cartesian paradigm. He reconciled the empirical inductive method of Bacon with the rational deductive method of Descartes, declaring both vital. The impact of the Cartesian-Newtonian world view has dominated Western Civilization in the 18th, 19th and early 20th Centuries — from specialization in health practice, to absence of ecological consideration in political and economic decision-making, to overwhelming successes in technology. Physics has been the basis for all other sciences which, in-turn, adhered to the mechanistic world view.

In the first half of the Twentieth Century, quantum and relativity physics shattered all the principal concepts of the Cartesian world view and Newtonian mechanics. During this period science moved from the Newtonian idea of the total predictability of nature into the new world of theoretical physics in which probability overshadows uncertainty. We have left behind the notion that the observer could objectively describe the observed. In quantum physics the act of observing creates relationship and affects the outcome of what is being observed.

In contrast to the Newtonian world view which held that the universe was a constant, both measurable and definable, the emerging paradigm recognizes that the universe is in a perpetual state of change. It also recognizes that matter and energy — consequently, body and mind — are dynamic aspects of the same thing. The new physics also reveals essential oneness. Our picture of the universe is becoming completely devoid of any isolated entities — even isolated energy fields — because, if all material objects are made of particles which are patterns of energy, and if all the forces which act between such objects are also made of particles which are patterns of energy, then the whole of creation must be a single, enormously intricate web of interconnected vibrational patterns.

Modern physics has clearly transcended the mechanistic Cartesian view of the world and is leading us to a holistic and intrinsically dynamic conception of the universe. It is inevitable that the other sciences will conform to the new paradigm.

A HOLISTIC PERSPECTIVE

Let us call this new view of science a *holistic* view, based on the premise that every part is an intrinsic part of the whole, interconnected, interrelated, and ultimately affecting and affected by all other parts. Conscious education shares this holistic view of reality with quantum physics.

In the foreword to Larry Dossey's book, *Space, Time and Medicine*, (1982) Fritjof Capra offers this thought:

> We live today in a globally interconnected world, in which biological, psychological, social, and environmental phenomena are all interdependent. To describe this world appropriately we need an ecological perspective, which the Cartesian world view does not offer. What we need, then, is a new vision of reality; a fundamental change in our thoughts, perceptions and values. The beginnings of this change, of the shift from the mechanistic to the holistic conception of reality, are already visible in all fields..."

An interesting metaphor for the new paradigm is holography. Holography is the study of pictures produced by using laser light to illuminate subject matter. The hologram is a special three-dimensional picture created by energy interference patterns. Holograms are truly three dimensional. One can walk all the way around the projected image and see it from above and below as if the image were real. But the most remarkable property of holograms is that one can cut away a small piece of the holographic film, hold it up to laser light, and still see an entire, intact three-dimensional image of the photographed object. Every piece contains the whole. Similarly, every cell within the human body contains the information to create an entire duplicate body (Gerber, 1988).

Since what happens in just a small fragment of the holographic energy interference pattern affects the entire structure simultaneously, there is an obvious relationship between all parts of the holographic universe. This conceptual change in scientific thinking is already having a profound effect in many areas. Let us briefly consider four fields that are demonstrating the impact of this holistic view of existence: medicine, business, religion and psychology.

Medicine

In the field of medicine, Larry Dossey (1982) suggests a "space-time model" which is aligned with the holistic view, and says that health is the harmony of fluid movement. It is not meant for human beings to be separated into parts in order for healing to occur. Rather, it is necessary to operate from the realization of the *process* of life — every step leading toward ultimate wholeness, i.e., health. Dossey's exemplification of the process orientation to health and disease demands that both healers and those wishing to be healed rethink their assumptions about the body and about their fundamental view of what constitutes health and disease. He explains:

> The space-time view of health and disease tells us that a vital part of the goal of every therapist is to help the sick person toward a reordering of his world view. We must help him realize that he is a *process* in space-time, not an isolated entity who is fragmented from the world of the healthy and who is adrift in flowing time, moving slowly toward extermination. To the extent that we accomplish this task we are healers.

Deepak Chopra (1989), endocrinologist and former chief of staff of New England Memorial Hospital in

Stoneham, Massachusetts, suggests:

> ...by following the story of neuro-peptides, we have ultimately arrived at a dramatic shift in world view. For the first time in the history of science, mind has a visible scaffold to stand upon... Before this, science declared that we are physical machines that have somehow learned to think...Now it dawns that we are thoughts that have learned to create a physical machine.

And we also cite the work of Richard Gerber who looks upon healers as spiritual scientists. Gerber (1988) observes:

> By realizing that humans are beings of energy, one can begin to comprehend new ways of viewing health and illness. This new Einsteinian viewpoint will not only give future doctors a unique perspective on the causes of disease, but also more effective ways by which human beings can be healed of their suffering.

Business

In the business field, top level management is moving towards people-centered models which offer opportunities for every part within the system to have meaningful input, recognizing that the whole is greater than the sum of its parts. These new techniques in management are already showing positive productivity results and are based on shared responsibility, shared leadership, cooperation and goodwill. Businesses are realizing 1) that every employee makes a difference and 2) that they have to include global impact in strategic plans, since every business is, essentially, an "employee" of a greater world group.

Willis Harman (1988) refers to the shift in business when he says:

> Fortune and Harvard Business Review have begun to publish articles referring to the use of hunches and intuition in business decision making. Management development courses in recent years have been increasingly overt about using such techniques as affirmation and inner imagery to remove barriers to creativity and intuition.

Perry Pascarella (1984), executive editor of *Industry Week*, writes:

> A quiet revolution is taking place...in the business corporation....Although we have been hearing more and more about corporate efforts in human resource development in recent years, we may miss the essential truth about what is happening: Individuals are awakening to the possibility of personal growth and finding opportunities to attain it.

These statements imply the realization of something beyond the five senses and the traditional models of leadership in business. Is it possible that the premise of conscious education, drawing forth the innate potential within every learner, is inherent in the fabric of the business revolution?

Religion

With respect to religion, numerous books and articles are being written to emphasize universality, i.e. looking at the sameness instead of the differences in beliefs. Religious leaders from around the world are demonstrating the willingness to come together and celebrate their similarities, seeking to unite humanity and move towards world peace. In 1989 the United Nations University for Peace hosted a global gathering which focused on a healing ecumenical religious ceremony. At the conference entitled, "Seeking the True Meaning of Peace," there was an interfaith experience which included world leaders and prayers from the following traditions: Buddhist, Catholic, Hindu, Islam, Bahá'í, Christian, Jewish and Indigenous Peoples.

The almost universally held religious belief that we are created from one source is aligned with the new scientific view. Indeed, we are finding that religion is impacted by this view because the recognition of holism brings to light the essential oneness of all beliefs. The metaphor of the wheel with many spokes can be used to illustrate similarities among religions. In this wheel each spoke represents a different religion. The center of the wheel can be thought of as Truth. As one proceeds along the path of any spoke towards the center, one gets closer to the ultimate Truth, yet at the same time, one gets closer to every other spoke (religion) as well.

Psychology

Psychology — literally the study of the soul — has long reflected the belief that we are, potentially, integrated human beings, i.e. an integration realized through the harmonization of physical, mental, emotional and spiritual human qualities. With the incorporation of transpersonal and esoteric psychology into the "spectrum of consciousness," a human being may now be looked upon as a soul who has chosen to evolve in the realm of physical existence, yet whose true essence or life resides on a level more subtle than the physical.

Authentic power exists inside, not outside. In a manner of speaking it is the soul and not the personality that is the inner authority. The old Cartesian scientific viewpoint ascribed to the idea of external power as the most important. The evolving scientific viewpoint substantiates that inner power is more *authentic*. One might extrapolate that this new scientific view is consistent with the transpersonal psychologists' idea that it is essential to align the soul and personality in order to know one's self and to fulfill one's life purpose.

Scott Peck (1978), author and psychotherapist, in concluding his definition of consciousness states that: *...when we become aware of a new truth, it is because we recognize it to be true; we re-know that which we knew all along.* The inference to an inner power or source is clear and speaks to authentic power existing inside. He goes on to suggest that:

> The fact that there exists beyond ourselves and our conscious will a powerful force that nurtures our growth and evolution is enough to turn our notions of self-insignificance topsy-turvy. For the existence of this force (once we perceive it) indicates with incontrovertible certainty that our human spiritual growth is of the utmost importance to something greater than ourselves.

RETHINKING EDUCATION

The shift in our scientific world view, from a separate one to a holistic one, also impacts education. Conventional educational methods *assume separateness:* the universe is made up of an infinite number of separate entities, things, events, having their own separate existence and identity and only accidentally or randomly relating to other "things" or "events."

Thus, in conventional education, there tend to be separate fields of study within a curriculum, with no apparent connection among them. Indeed, there are separate classes for everything, and there is the generally accepted attitude that each body of knowledge is a distinct and separate "subject" composed of objective, undeniable facts which can be transmitted by teachers talking to students.

Conscious education, paralleling the shifting scientific view, assumes wholeness: *everything is connected to everything else.* This "new" assumption opens the door for an education based on a holistic perspective — a learning environment in which everything is relevant to everything else, and every learner plays a significant role. An opportunity is thus created to shift from information-based to learner-based education.

Edward Clark (1992), in-line with the new scientific view, offers an in-depth look at old and new assumptions in education. He states:

> When one examines these new assumptions thoughtfully, it seems clear that what is required is nothing short of a new educational paradigm — a vision and a set of fundamental principles which emerge from the "assumption of wholeness." The simple reality is that if educational

reform is to be substantive and long lasting, it must be holistic. The holistic perspective recognizes a new set of assumptions about both the nature of children and the nature of the learning environment.

Clark goes on to suggest that, based on the initial shift from separateness to wholeness, a whole series of assumptions in education emerges. *Brain antagonistic assumptions* are those associated with the old thinking. These assumptions include:

- Intelligence exists in a limited, "fixed" amount that can be accurately measured with a mathematical formula.
- Intelligence can be defined and measured exclusively in terms of mathematical and verbal skills.
- The ability to remember and recall is a valid measure of intelligence and a good predictor of success.
- The only way of knowing, i.e., acquiring knowledge, is through our physical senses.

Brain compatible assumptions are those associated with wholeness, and Clark takes us from the old assumptions to the new:

- Human potential may be essentially unlimited.
- Intelligence is multi-dimensional and can be expressed in a variety of ways.
- Children learn in different ways, at different rates, and express their learning in a wide variety of ways.
- Most "youth at risk" are global learners who require a "big picture" context for understanding and learning.

As education takes its place in the evolving paradigm, conscious education offers a contextual framework based on brain compatible assumptions as aligned with unity and wholeness. The learner is encouraged to fully participate in the process of expressing the qualities of the soul while crossing the bridge in a unique and meaningful way.

Chapter Five

COSMIC LAWS / PRINCIPLES IN EDUCATION

One of the most urgent endeavours to be undertaken on behalf of the reconstruction of society is the reconstruction of education. It must be brought about by giving the children the environment which is adapted to their life....following the guide of the cosmic laws.

Maria Montessori (1955)

What are the strands that weave the tapestry of spirituality in education?

What is the impact of cosmic laws and principles on education? How can educators utilize this information? In the authors' view, all of life is based on the underlying influence of these laws and principles and thus, they are essential to conscious learning as well.

At the core of the shift in the scientific view of reality, leading to the recognition of the brain compatible assumptions in education, lie the basic cosmic laws and principles. The formerly separate parts of our educational approach can now be seen as interconnected, interrelated parts of a dynamic whole — one education system serving the needs of the learner. This will become even more apparent as the reader moves through Chapter Six.

The basic laws and principles which we summarize below offer the possibility for truly interdisciplinary study, an integrated curriculum, and a system of education that is like the interaction of subatomic particles, a continuous dance of energy.

COSMIC LAWS AND PRINCIPLES

The dance of energy — that which stems from cosmic law — provides new organizing principles for understanding existence as well as our interactions from the microcosm to the macrocosm. These are not new ideas, yet are cogent to the emerging new paradigms in business, religion, medicine, psychology, education and virtually all disciplines. Here we present some of these laws and how they are integral to the development of a structure for conscious education.

1. **Everything is alive,** from the smallest organism known to humankind, to the planet and to the universe itself. Zukav (1991), in the <u>Proceedings of the 3rd International Forum on New Science</u>, points out that human beings are no longer limited to perception through the five senses. Rather, we are becoming multisensory:

> That Universe, of which our physical reality is a part, is alive. This is the fundamental perception of the multisensory human: the Universe is much larger than the five sensory experience of physical reality, and it is alive. There is nothing in the Universe that is not alive. Life pervades everything. There is nothing but Life.

As we leave behind the confines of an existence based on the five senses, we encounter intuition and non-physical reality. The inner knowing and multi-sensory perception referred to in the section on psychology lead to the ability to develop authentic power through responsible choice. Empirical science and education must meet the need, in Zukav's words, *to recognize the existence of non-physical reality*. This is necessary if education is to address the inner self — the true learner.

2. **Matter and spirit are the same energy,** vibrating at different frequencies. Matter is spirit vibrating at its lowest level, and spirit is matter vibrating at its highest level (Blavatsky, 1888). Again, Zukav offers a clear explanation when he says,

> The singularly new perception of the multisensory human is this: SPIRIT IS REAL. The recognition, acceptance, and inquiry into the nature of existence and intelligence that is both real and nonphysical is the foundation of the science that is now longing to be born.

Zukav further states that, *As our species becomes multisensory and individuals increasingly recognize themselves and others as souls evolving through experiences within the learning environment of the five senses, the intellectual center of gravity shifts from the mind to the heart.* As this shift occurs, a heart-centered education develops — in-line with learner-centered education, emphasizing the drawing forth of the innate knowingness and potential within every learner.

Scientific inquiry is moving towards the realization that matter and spirit are one substance — the frequency determining the density. Conscious education is based on the integration of soul and personality, recognizing that they are one substance.

The visible light spectrum, i.e., that range of frequency vibrations that the human eye and brain know as vision, represents a very small portion of a continuum — an infinite scale. Beyond this portion in one direction are ultra violet radiation, x-rays, micro waves, and more. Beyond this portion in the other direction are infrared rays, low frequency radiation, and more. In other words, with the physical eye, we only see a fraction of what actually exists.

So, physicists agree that everything is energy, that everything is in a constant state of motion and that the part of the known and measurable vibrational spectrum that we use to validate our reality is incredibly narrow. Is it possible that reality extends beyond the five physical senses? Yes. Is it possible that human thought itself is a vibrational frequency? Yes. Is it possible that the upper end of the vibrational spectrum is higher than we can now measure? Yes. Is it conceivable that matter and spirit are simply different vibrations on this scale of frequencies that describes all of life? Yes.

3. **The Law of Manifestation.** All of manifestation is energy, and energy follows thought. We are the creators of our world. We manifest our own reality. We are ultimately interconnected and interdependent co-creators with the responsibility for right thinking, right speech and right action. Our very existence is a creation, and we consciously and unconsciously *create* at every moment of our lives. Thoughts are things, and thoughts create movement towards creation.

Many people seem to believe that they do not have an effect on the world and, in fact, that the environment controls them. Quite the opposite is the case, and, according to Zukav (1991):

> This is the most fundamental shift that science will encounter as it transits from the special limiting case of the old empirical science with its singular focus on the constitution of physical reality to the new emerging science: Our inner

dynamics create the world, the world does not
create our inner dynamics.

The recognition of this law is empowering. It encourages one to operate from a heart-centered position of love,
trust, compassion and the good of the whole. Otherwise,
one may operate under the false premise that *"They* made
me do it!" One may lash out in anger at something that
"makes me angry," whereas in actuality one is feeding and
manifesting the anger.

Conscious education encourages individuals to learn
to live from their inner authentic power base, the soul,
expressed through their personality, and to make choices to
direct their energy in accordance with an understanding of
the Law of manifestation. The learners may then cross the
bridge as responsible co-creators.

4. **The Law of Cause and Effect**. This law is familiar to
us because it is a part of Newton's laws of motion. However,
the physical law of cause and effect is the reflection of a
more comprehensive non-physical dynamic. Every cause
has an effect, and every effect has a cause. Each cause and its
effect are, in essence, one and the same dynamic.

Everything we think, say or do has a reaction. Within
every situation we reap our past, and with every action we
build our future. In order to fully understand this law, one
must accept that humans exist beyond the five senses of the
physical world. Causes have outer effects, and the consequences of individual choices are reflected not only in this
life — but are carried from one life to another as the soul
evolves.

Intentional choice is a key, for it is the intention that
determines the consequence of the action. To yell at someone may be harmful when the intention is to hurt for

personal, angry reasons. However, to yell at someone in order to warn of impending danger will result in positive feedback.

The Law of Cause and Effect is integral to conscious education. Every action has a consequence, and the *intention* of the action is directly related to that consequence. In every moment we are faced with choices, and those choices shape our future. All of life presents such learning experiences. This law is the ultimate teacher of responsibility.

5. **The Law of Attraction**. This law describes the incredible force of attraction that holds everything together, from our solar system to our human bodies. The essence of this law is to blend the soul and personality through the force of attraction.

In reality, the Law of Attraction is a reflection of the Law of love, with two primary components: radiation and magnetism. Radiation operates through expansion, or emanation of certain qualities. It includes, or fuses, everything in its sphere of influence. For example, an educator who radiates qualities of the soul — goodness, beauty and truth — infuses the environment with those qualities, drawing forth the souls of learners within that sphere of influence. Magnetism operates between two points, creating a magnetic flow of energy between them.

The Law of *Magnetic* Attraction is at work in our everyday lives. Like attracts like. We live in a world in which those people who are seeking to do a certain thing are inevitably attracted to like-minded and like-hearted individuals, and together, they participate in their mutual creation. *What we are is what we attract.* If young people begin to experience and understand that their personal world of conflict and chaos is a self-attracted world, they will choose to change their behavior.

This law allows the conscious educator to realize the significance of the quality of inclusiveness in the learning environment. Everything one expresses touches and effects everyone in the learning environment.

6. The Law of Love. Love manifests through space and time throughout the universe. The Law of Love is the law of the system — the impelling motive for all manifestation. Love conditions everything and keeps order. Love bears and perfects all. Love builds forms that hold inner life and love disrupts those same forms in order that life may progress (Bailey, 1925).

The Law of Love transmutes desires. This is clearly visible when we look at the various expressions of love. For example, as a personality we go through stages of selfish, personal love to love of family and friends, gradually realizing an expression of the soul in the love of humanity or group love. When learners are recognized as soul-infused personalities in potential, then love takes on the quality of the heart. Love goes beyond an emotional framework and is service-oriented.

Conscious education is aligned with the Law of Love and is synonymous with heart-centered education. The educator, who identifies with spirit, develops soul relationships with learners on the physical plane, leading to the establishment of right human relations.

7. The Law of Right Human Relations is a keynote for harmony within the human family. Right human relations is the act of living harmoniously in cooperation with the planet. It includes interpersonal and intrapersonal ways of knowing and being. This law might be called the *science* of right human relations, since its practice brings into effect the best of the laws previously discussed.

The practice of right human relations begins with the self. Developing a healthy relationship with oneself, physically, emotionally, mentally and spiritually is a prerequisite for healthy interactions with others. Self-respect leads to respect of others; self love and understanding leads to loving and understanding others. As we cross the bridge toward autonomous freedom, this principle is paramount to a developing sense of responsibility and independence, leading to a healthy relationship with self, others and all life on the planet.

Inherent in the science of right human relations is the Principle of Goodwill. Goodwill is love in action to transform the world. It begins with the *will-to-good*, activating spirit into matter. It translates spirit into practical life as an act of doing good will. Simply put, do unto life as you would have life do unto you.

COSMIC LAWS AND PRINCIPLES IN THE LEARNING ENVIRONMENT

As educators embody these laws and principles, an inherent understanding and appreciation for life emerges. Perhaps the most important quality in a teacher is authenticity — operating as the inner self, expressed through the personality. When an educator is authentic, learning environments are consciously created and infused with soul energy, affording learners opportunities to nurture and unfold *their* spirit.

In a setting where the overriding quality is authenticity, curriculum is naturally seen as part of the larger picture — part of the oneness of all life. In this setting, learners discover that their lives and attitudes make a difference, that the path to world peace is to have peace in their hearts, and to act with goodwill.

Responsibility, a keynote of the soul, is naturally evoked when individuals recognize that their thoughts, words and actions have an effect on both themselves and their environment. A learning atmosphere that is reflective of these cosmic laws and principles encourages learners to take their place with authentic confidence and understanding as they journey across the bridge.

Humanity has reached a stage of consciousness that enables the understanding of how all life on this planet is interconnected. Now there is a possibility for educators to model this concept by developing structures that support this understanding. As our environmental concerns pull us together externally, so our educational concerns can pull us together internally — through a spiritual perspective. Through this unity within our diversity there is the true possibility to forge new territory — to be no longer separate — and to create a global concept in recognizing that we are all members of the human family.

In building educational programs with spirituality as a foundational concept, the intention is to promote the twin freedoms of individual creative expression and social responsibility. Inculcation of dogmatic theological and denominational teachings are *not* the aim. Spirituality does not become a subject matter, but is rather the thread that runs through and permeates all activity. It is the contextual framework — the tapestry — for an understanding of and participation in this incredible process of conscious evolution.

Education is a key to change. How we use that key will materially impact the future of our children and our planet. Awareness is the first step on the road to change. It is time to stop building on old models and become visionary leaders in education in order to transform and to fashion these new outcomes that we know are possible. What will further life on this planet in a healthy and harmonious way? How can the educational process support the concepts outlined in this chapter? Individual success and national well-being are aspects of a bigger picture, a picture of individual excellence within the group we call humanity — a picture of every human being and nation offering its best for the good of the whole.

How can education help create a cosmic view? How can education help children understand the big picture? The authors believe that it can be brought about through education with a purpose and a vision: *spirituality in education, a drawing forth of the spirit*. Education is meant to be alive and joyful, for all of life is about learning, and life seen through spiritual eyes is deeply joyful.

As we approach education, so will we approach life. Education for life, based on cosmic laws and principles, fosters both personal and planetary fulfillment. It weaves the fabric of the form in Part II of this book.

CONCLUSION TO PART I, PROCESS

In Part I we have explored the process of education through the spectrum of conscious evolution. Attributes, the innate human ways of knowing, include exploration/curiosity, observation, imagination and creativity, intuition, communication and collaboration, responsiveness and self-perfection. These attributes are in potential at birth. They are the vehicle for human interaction with the inner and outer world. When people are provided opportunities to live out these attributes, they are empowered to cross the bridge towards autonomous freedom.

The bridge reveals the relationship among freedom, responsibility, independence, trust and spirituality. These ways of being are the avenues of human interaction that foster the full potential of human attributes. Set against the background of the cosmic principles discussed in this chapter, we see that the interaction of these concepts provides the environment for conscious education process (Figure 5.1).

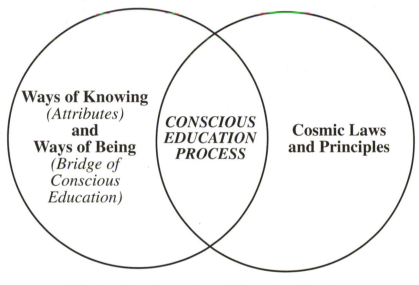

Figure 5.1 Conscious Education Process

PART II
FORM

Chapter Six

CREATING FORM

*The right kind of education means the awakening
of intelligence, the fostering of an integrated life,
and only such education can create a new culture
and a peaceful world; but to bring about this new
education we must make a fresh start on an en-
tirely different basis.*

J. Krishnamurti (1953)

The path across the bridge towards autonomous freedom is accelerated by improving the process of interaction
between individuals and themselves, individuals and parents, and individuals and teachers/facilitators/mentors.
This journey is imbued with the inspiration of conscious
living and life purpose. If the purpose of education is to
enable the rising generation to fulfill their potential and
become responsible, fully functioning members of society,
then education must provide the modes of learning that
empower such progress.

The great teachings of the world tell us that in the
beginning there was pure energy. Through time this energy
differentiated and materialized into form. If energy is to
process as matter is to form, we might say that process
creates the structure for form.

Having defined conscious education process as the
intersection of human ways of knowing and being with
cosmic principles, it is now time to turn our attention to
conscious education form. *What are the modes of learning that
shift education from the industrial paradigm of the Cenozoic to the*

transformational paradigm of the Ecozoic? How do these ingredi-ents or methods support global interdependence and universal responsibility? Conscious education form (Figure 6.1) is represented by six modes of learning or motifs. Set into a star this vision calls for a harmony between the personal and the global as well as the material and the spiritual.

These motifs are:

Multiple Age Grouping: To allow for individual differ-ences, foster peer tutoring, promote collaboration and cooperation, and help in the development of self-directed learning.

Altruistic Learning: To enable learners to develop community. This is the fostering of local, national and world citizenship through pro-social behavior.

Reflective Learning: To develop independent think-ing and recognize innate consciousness.

Experiential Learning: To foster personal empower-ment and social responsibility.

Systemic Learning: To underscore the relationship between unity and diversity, matter and energy; and, to emphasize the interrelationship among all disciplines, matter and energy.

Transpersonal Learning: To nurture the intuitive, imaginative and creative capacity of each individual and to help in the development of self-understanding and life purpose.

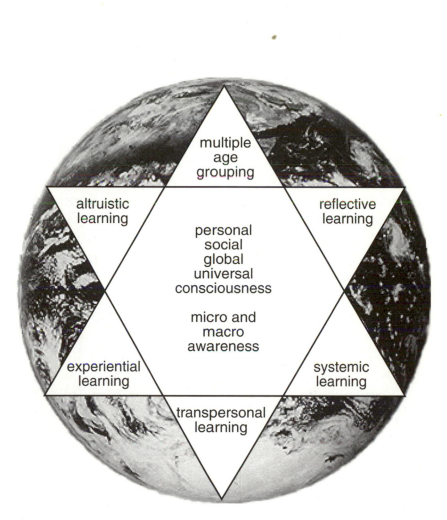

Figure 6.1 Conscious Education Model of Form

MULTIPLE AGE GROUPING

*Any method which classifies children according
to temperament and aptitude merely emphasizes
their differences; it breeds antagonism, encourages divisions in society and does not help to
develop integrated human beings.*

Krishnamurti (1953)

Our present system of graded schools is an outgrowth
of the industrial paradigm. These early schools created an
ordered and well disciplined society — one that would
compliment the needs of the factory system. Knowledge
was placed into fixed categories and information was given
out in "assembly line" fashion, complete with mandatory
time increments. There was subject specialization, rote
repetitive work and clear hierarchical roles with defined
obedience/authority relationships. Learners were organized by age into a structured sequence of grades on the
premise that knowledge grows at a constant rate and is
acquired incrementally. All this was necessary to power
the industrial economy.

We are living in the post industrial era — the age of
information and services — and people are entering society
with the wrong skills and abilities. The traditional age-
grade vertical curricula organizational scheme has outlived
its usefulness. According to Miller (1989),

> Learners benefit from working in group situ-
> ations where many competencies, ages and
> points of view are represented ...whole class
> instruction, where students of differing abili-
> ties and ages work together, leads toward
> improved student relations. When students

> are taught by (specific) grade levels, a status
> hierarchy often occurs between the grades.
> When grades are combined and taught to-
> gether, this hierarchy breaks down...

Developmental psychology provides a window for us to envision a healthy system of grouping learners. Through an analysis of cognitive, moral and spiritual development we can see how individuals within certain specific age ranges have more or less the same capacity and potential. When learners are grouped according to multiple ages, a dynamic tension is created which enhances the learners' ability to grow independently and collectively. Multiple age grouping:

> allows for individual differences,
> fosters peer tutoring,
> promotes collaboration and cooperation, and
> helps in the development of self-directed learning.

Individual Differences

Because of our psycho-biological nature human beings share a common heritage and a common bond. But we are all different. From birth to death we cross the bridge toward autonomous freedom at different biological and psychological rates.

When we discuss individual differences, we are not only addressing variations among people, but variations within each person. Any plan for education needs to address both variations. When we pay attention to our own rhythm we notice how there are times for being still and there are times for forward movement. A healthy learning environment respects both kinds of differences and supports the individual's effort to walk one's own path.

In multi-graded classrooms learners can progress at their own rate without the comparisons that arise in the traditional class. Teachers are able to help each person according to his or her individual needs. This process necessitates trust. Some children blossom into reading at age six while others as late as eight or even nine. Who is to say what is right or wrong? Children of eight years that explode into reading do not "miss" anything. In the multi-graded classroom there are activities across the curriculum that engage the non-reader. In fact, these children usually excel in some other form — perhaps mathematics or art!

Peer Tutoring

One of the delightful outcomes of the multi-grade experience is the development of peer tutoring. A well balanced heterogeneous classroom contains learners that span several years within a particular developmental construct. In Montessori environments this span is identified by three year increments. Conceptually, the oldest third of the class has been together for more than two years; the middle third for more than a year; and the youngest third are the newcomers. In the best situations the teacher is also a stabilizing influence remaining with the class for a minimum three year cycle. An ongoing teacher's dialogue with children might go something like this:

> There is so much to learn that it is impossible for me to give every lesson to every one of you. You too have some responsibility for teaching. When others want a lesson, try to help them.

Teaching reinforces learning. It solidifies concepts that are loosely threaded together and it creates in-depth knowledge. It is in the teaching that real learning occurs, including insight, awareness and further application. When children teach each other they have the unique ability to find just the right amount of words — those that are meaningful and necessary. Adults tend to do too much explaining.

Peer tutoring also strengthens the development of community. Through lateral empowerment learners come together to explore, communicate and collaborate. Younger persons appreciate the contribution of their "elders," and a caring, supportive atmosphere is created.

Cooperation and Collaboration

Humanity has evolved as one of the advanced life forms on this planet because it discovered that survival and success depend on its ability to work together for the common good. Modern education still echoes to the commands of, *"Do your own work!" "Keep your eyes on your own paper!" "No talking!"* This attitude is poor preparation for life in the real world which is highly dependent on people to people experience. Throughout schooling, learners are subjected to the subliminal message that discovery and knowledge is personal. This leads toward an egocentric world view and challenges the individual's ability to integrate into society. Ostensibly, these attitudes became doctrine in order to instill competitiveness and to measure individual capacity. Successful experiences in the real world are usually cooperative and it is the capacity of the group that is more significant than the individual.

Since cooperation and collaboration are innate attributes of humanity, they should flourish in the healthy learning environment. In the heterogeneous classroom individuals work together for the common good. As the learning stretches across a multiple year increment, individuals get to know each other beyond the superficial and are encouraged to work cooperatively as an extension of social living. It is in this capacity for collaboration that interest and enthusiasm replaces the externalization of rewards. Cooperation is a natural human attribute that occurs spontaneously where there is freedom, trust and responsibility.

Today, *cooperative learning* is being popularized as a new educational methodology. It is a learning technique in which individuals work in small groups to help one another master concepts and is seen as a tool to remedy a host of educational problems. Cooperative learning methods share the idea that students work together to learn and are responsible for one another's learning as well as their own. Cooperative learning is a vast improvement over other techniques and methods, yet it is mere window dressing for the changes that are required. In many applications of the techniques, teachers still remain in the center, directing, rather than facilitating experience. What is needed is wholesale re-conceptualization that begins with process and extends through form.

Self Directed Learning

The bridge for conscious education is constructed for the self-directed learner. It presupposes that each person's journey is driven by an inner knowing. Differences that exist in a multi-grade classroom put a constant demand on the teacher's time. Multigrade teachers, therefore, must be well organized, resourceful and able to help students develop self direction.

Think for a moment. As a teacher, you have 25 children in your class of nine, ten and eleven year olds. You are working with a group of six children who are learning about operations with decimal numbers. It is a very detailed lesson that will take about one hour. You know that if you are constantly distracted by the others, the lesson will lose its impact. What are the other 19 children doing while you are involved with this group?

If the facilitator is well prepared, then most of the learners will work independently, either by themselves or in small groups. Being well prepared connotes the development of a classroom environment that supports freedom of choice in an atmosphere of personal responsibility. It means reviewing activity or work plans with each child on a regular basis; and it means trusting that spontaneous discoveries are made when learners are allowed to explore on their own.

Self-directed learners take initiative, accept responsibility and see challenges as opportunities. They are people who feel empowered.

ALTRUISTIC LEARNING

There seems to be little question that altruism is a powerful source of energy in human affairs. It has been argued that the innate altruistic drive allowed humanity to pursue survival at the highest levels. According to Richard Leakey (1978):

> People help each other all the time, and they are motivated to, not only by repeated calculations of the ultimate benefit to themselves through returned favors, but because they are psychologically motivated to do so. This is precisely what one would expect; over countless generations natural selection favored the emergence of emotions that made reciprocal altruism work, emotions such as "sympathy," "gratitude," "guilt," and "moral indignation."

At best, our survival could be approached through the window of community, yet today a majority of people live solely for personal or nuclear family well-being. Except in remote pockets, people have moved away from their communal centers. In the short run this apparently satisfies immediate needs. However, it does not consider the greater whole — the interconnectedness of everything and the evolutionary process. A short term approach to survival eventually leads to the deterioration of society. The environmental crisis is a perfect example of how the erosion of altruism is already spelling doom for our species.

Early people knew that their personal well-being was tied to the well-being of the community. They lived it at the concrete level of satisfying primary needs. We have lost that connection. Our species must realize that the welfare of the individual is dependent on the welfare of the community, of the nation, and of the world. Well-being is a direct result of an altruistic society — a society that feels the spiritual and moral responsibility to care for the welfare of the whole.

Selfishness and egoistic behavior have left an indelible mark on the Earth's landscape. We can see this with environmental problems. They portray how the self interest of individuals who are *not* concerned for the welfare of others is destroying our species. The rising generation needs to realize that the welfare of the individual is based on the well-being of the whole. This is part of the conscious evolutionary path and is inherent in the Bridge of Conscious Education.

Development of Community

The word community is derived from the Latin *communis*, meaning "common state." To develop community in the school or in society there must be a common state or ground. Common ground emerges through dialogue, acceptance and appreciation. It leads to citizenship.

We educate to prepare good citizens ...not just "academic" citizens, but individuals who can make a contribution to society. For hundreds of thousands of years communities were built around the extended family and clan for the satisfaction of primary needs. Young people grew up surrounded by community action and decision making, and in time, took their place as citizens of the group. The community process was lived and experienced. Young people today have no such frame of reference. The extended family has virtually disappeared and the "community" is so large — even in small towns — that there is a disorientation around what makes it all work. How can our children develop a sense of community without living models?

Genuine community arises out of group interdependence and mutual respect. It is supported by reciprocal altruism and is sustained by heart energy. Our schools must re-create community as a living experience for young people. We can do this by creating learning environments that foster pro-social behavior and by modeling indigenous people practices as still held by traditional elders. According to Van Oudenhoven (1982),

> Pro-social behavior relates to attitudes such
> as interest in others, helping and caring be-
> havior, empathy, altruism, concern for others,
> and perspective-taking and the like.

Community-building is the climate of necessity under which a new world order can begin to emerge.

In recalling one of our teaching experiences with a nine to twelve year old class we remember using a democratic system for dealing with issues, feelings, suggestions and "great" ideas. It is the "classroom meeting" or "pow wow."

Issues were debated about fairness. Feelings and strong emotions were very often expressed. Right and wrong sometimes became ambiguous. Truth seemed to reveal itself. And there was an unexpressed undercurrent of love and respect. These children had developed a supportive community based on the mutual concern for each other's well-being.

Experiences in community are a prerequisite for good citizenship. When individuals are in an environment that applauds pro-social behavior they develop moral feelings of compassion and empathy as well as respect for rules — not a law and order imposed by the hierarchy, but one born in the depths of an inner knowing that *rules* are needed to protect relationships and the common good. Community and good citizenship is nurtured by supporting the individual's effort to climb the ladder of moral understanding.

Education aids this understanding by creating a climate for dialogue, social intercourse and action. Dialogue enables the individual to feel a sense of value. It is empowering because the Self is reinforced. Social intercourse is the next level of dialogue. It enables people to work together for the common good. Action reinforces and validates values. It is the vehicle for transforming thought into reality.

If schools exist to prepare good citizens they have an obligation to create community at all levels of experience. For the youngest learners this may mean within their own classroom. For older children, dialogue, social intercourse and action moves outward toward school, locality, city, state, nation and globe. This is not a linear process. A young person can simultaneously have a sense of community in the locality while demonstrating compassion and empathy for global situations.

REFLECTIVE LEARNING

Self-reflected consciousness is the spearhead of evolution.

Peter Russell (1983)

When you discover that *you know* you know it builds self-esteem and is self-empowering. The purpose of reflective learning is to aid each person in this process. To "reflect" is a derivative of the Latin, *reflectere,* meaning to "bend back." When we take opportunities to reflect, we are literally bending back to our subconscious, to our intuitive knowing and to our soul. Reflective thinking allows the learner to survey purpose.

Reflective learning promotes the expansion of consciousness because it provides a safe space for learners to explore their higher selves. It supports independent thinking as it enables learners to discover and create their own meaning, thereby reinforcing self concept.

We are reminded of the remarks of an 11 year who persistently questioned the validity of what she was asked to do: *Why is this important? How does it relate to real life?* Conscious education requires a shift from environments that are insensitive to these questions to environments that see these reflective questions as the very heart of learning and the beginning of understanding.

Components of reflective learning include: the art of questioning, reflection and creativity, and interviewing.

Art of Questioning

Questioning in school often follows the old industrial model. It is used to prove "power over," and is a tool to control and to draw "right" and "wrong" responses. As the old Newtonian scientific foundation that supports this way of thinking has broken down, its usefulness in our everyday lives has diminished.

Questioning can model a transformed view when it helps learners understand that a variety of solutions may be valid in any particular situation, when it enables them to access their inner knowing, when it evokes inquiry and exploration, and when it taps into the imagination.

The process of reflection is more beneficial to the learner than actually having "acceptable" or "right" answers. Reflective learning invites learners to share in the education process, and to value their input alongside the teacher. The learner and teacher join in the process of inquiry, making the shared understanding accessible and valuable to both.

Carin and Sund (1971) explain that a good teacher, in private conversations with students, might ask some of the following kinds of questions:

> Where do you come from?
> Where were you born?
> Where do you live?
> What do you want to learn?
> What would you like to learn?
> What do you want to become?
> What do you think would be the best way to become that?
> If you could do anything you wanted today, what would you do?
> How do you feel about that?
> What makes you sad?
> What makes you happy?
> What do you think are your strongest attributes?
> What do you do well?
> What do you need to improve?

How can I help?
What's great about this course (class)?
What's wrong with this course (class)?
How could I improve as a teacher?
What do we need to do to improve this course, school, etc.?

Reflective questioning brings to consciousness things that you have not said, but *you know* you know. When they are non-judgmental and inclusive, questions have the capacity to elicit inner knowing. In reflective relationships between teachers and learners, learners are empowered to explore their inner and outer selves, while teachers are empowered to be who they are.

When learners pose questions, teachers are presented a golden opportunity for reflective response. For example:

Learner: Why is the sky blue?
Teacher: Why do you think its blue?
Learner: Because light is blue?
Teacher: I wonder what might make light blue?
Learner: I don't know.
Teacher: Well let's find out together; or perhaps we can get someone else to help us find an answer. Maybe you can find out for yourself.

In this hypothetical exchange, the teacher advances to a certain layer of the dialogue and moves from reflective questioning to supportive facilitating. It is the *questions* that stimulate learners' desires to "find their answer."

Reflection and Creativity

Developing creative abilities opens us to increasing experience; the more we are involved in a creative enterprise, the more creative we become. An awareness that we are creative builds our self image. Reflective questions that are open-ended and not value-ridden, stimulate creative activity.

People are creative when they use their minds to produce something uniquely new. This may be a sketch, song, idea, story or any new synthesis. What kinds of questions stimulate creativity? Certainly not ones that require a memory response! Questions that are preceded by, *I wonder why.....?* or, *Could it be that...?* or, *What do you think will happen if.....?* stir multi-level thinking and thus foster creativity.

Interviewing

Reflective questioning can be taught. Teachers can help learners understand the process by "teaching" the skills of interviewing. We recall one of the games played while teaching a class of nine to eleven year olds. After lunch there was a fantasy visit from an extra terrestrial being. The children loved to be questioned about life on Earth. They would respond to questions like: *What do you like best on Earth? What kind of problems are there on this planet? Do you know some of the solutions? Tell me something about your deepest thoughts as an Earth citizen!* Then it was the children's turn. They might ask this "visitor" about its home. One could either respond in metaphor or make a funny game out of the experience.

The point is that interviewing can be a non-judgmental activity that empowers learners to explore the deepest part of their inner knowing and innate understanding.

As teachers model the interview process with learners, the learners begin to understand how they can utilize the technique for their own purpose. During a visit to a school in Oslo, Norway, a nine year old was observed forging a hat out of paper and tape. On it he wrote the word, "PRESS."

On his desk he placed the sign, "CITY DESK." He and a colleague, with pencils wedged above their ears, walked throughout the classroom interviewing other children and the teacher for their class newsletter. It provided a wonderful opportunity to teach the art of asking interesting questions — ones that require reflective thinking and learning.

While reflective learning represents only one of the conscious education motifs, it is the thread that creates the interconnection of the star (Figure 6.1). Reflective learning is integral to 'multiple age grouping, as well as altruistic, experiential, systemic and transpersonal learning. Reflective questions create an atmosphere where conscious learning can flourish.

EXPERIENTIAL LEARNING

> *The idea of using the present simply to get ready for the future contradicts itself. It omits, and even shuts out, the very conditions by which a person can be prepared for his future. We always live at the time we live and not at some future time, and only by extracting at each present time the full meaning of each present experience are we prepared for doing the same thing in the future. This is the only preparation which in the long run amounts to anything.*
>
> John Dewey (1938)

Experience has been the basis of learning from the inception of humanity's appearance on earth. However, in the last few hundred years there has been an overeager embrace of the rational, scientific and technological. Our concept of the learning process has been distorted, first by rationalism and later by behaviorism. We have lost touch with our own experience as a source of personal learning and development, and in that process, lost that centeredness necessary to counterbalance the "scientific" centeredness that has permeated life in the 19th and 20th Century.

Experience is an act of connecting head and heart. It is a manifestation of will enabling individuals to build an integrated cycle of knowing. Where there is no experience there is no energy, no spark of creation. Where there *is* experience, creative energy naturally bridges process and form.

Aspects of experiential learning include:

- Active experimentation and discovery to bring about awareness and meaning.

- Concrete actions within the environment in order to form abstractions.

- Productive involvement and participation in the social life of the community.

Experimentation and Discovery

Experimentation is the application of principles or theories arrived at through concrete experience. A healthy learning environment enables the learner to take actions and arrive at abstractions through experimentation. Students in the Montessori elementary class use a material known as the "chequerboard" to learn long multiplication. During initial contacts with this material the child places sets of bead bars on the board in such a way that the geometric form of multiplication can be internalized. At this stage of the work, correct answers are not as important as understanding the process. After working at this concrete level for some time, the child begins to reflect on the experience. This is followed by a period of theorizing or abstracting. Now the child thinks, *I wonder if I could apply what I know about this material to perform long multiplication abstractly.* Experimentation begins and the child discovers that there is no longer a need for the concrete material and can rely on his or her own internalized process.

Action and Abstraction

Group discussions and debates help students prepare for their role in society. These experiences not only provide an opportunity to develop communication and interaction skills, but give students direct encounters with the decision-making process. Cooperative work and collaborative decision-making is experienced through active participation. In a healthy educational setting learners form small groups for research projects. They divide the work based on individual interest and skill. One child might find all the books, another do the writing, another the drawing and another cut out pictures from magazines. The group works together, making all the necessary decisions. Upon completion they give a presentation to the whole class.

Effective problem-solving is a dynamic process helping students understand that a myriad of solutions may exist side by side for any one particular situation. Concrete experiences of this nature assist in forming an adult personality that can look beyond the limited thinking that "one person can be responsible for everything." There is a realization that the whole is greater than the sum of the parts and that everyone plays a unique and significant role. Carl Rogers (1969) suggests that classrooms change their focus:

> When a teacher is concerned with the facilitation of learning rather than with the function of teaching, he organizes his time and efforts very differently than the conventional teacher... he concentrates on providing all kinds of resources which will give his students experiential learning relevant to their needs.

Experiential learning that involves participation in group process is one such valuable resource.

Social Life Involvement

In Montessori's (1937) scenario for secondary education she explains:

> The essential reform is this: to put the adolescent on the road to achieving economic independence. We might call it a school of experience in the elements of social life.

What she describes is a rural residential community of adults and adolescents who live and work together in a self-sufficient community, experiencing the supreme reality of social life.

The realities of our time require a more acceptable, more realistic approach. An urban setting can provide two alternatives for community involvement. The first is the establishment of a student owned and operated "cottage industry." The second involves a program for student internships. Through internships or apprenticeships young people explore social life at its core and begin to realize their own competence and capacity for contributing in the adult world. In *Touching the World*, Arms and Denman (1975) describe the goals of the internship program at "Kaleidoscope," a community involvement project of the Philadelphia public schools:

> ...the interns' involvement was geared to something quite different than "choice preparation" for future work. Rather, their involvement was intended as a form of living and growing experience aimed at meeting their most immediate needs as people.

Involvement in the social life of the community extends to elementary children as well. They need opportunities to explore society. This not only answers an internal need of children to explore beyond the classroom, but gives them more data to construct their own world view and prepare them for "going out" as an adolescent.

At the preschool level social life experiences connect the child to the real-to-life home environment. Children learn to care for themselves, to do simple and complex chores (e.g. preparing food, folding, sweeping, etc.) as well as the social graces such as greeting a visitor, shaking hands or how to ask for things in a polite manner.

Those schools that help connect students to the social life of the community are contributing to the development of an integrated personality. Once we move from the limited notion of the 19th century school, education will regain its experiential heritage and become more conscious.

SYSTEMIC LEARNING

Today we live in a globally interconnected world in which biological, psychological, social and environmental systems are all interdependent. To understand this world appropriately, we need an integrated perspective which reductionist thinking simply does not offer.

Fritjof Capra (1982)

For hundreds of years humanity subjected reality to the pragmatic tests of reductionism. This approach has now been shattered as new scientific discoveries reveal the complexification of reality. Complexity assumes that reality is open-ended and web-like, with multiple interacting forces. This expanded notion of reality is fundamental to the emerging systemic world view.

When asked to describe a system, young people usually give examples like, the "solar" system or the "digestive" system. *What is a system?* They reply, *"It is a group of things working together."* Add to this a sense of wholeness and we see how systems are integrated wholes and systems theory looks at the world in terms of the inter-relatedness and interdependence of all phenomena. Conscious education is systemic because it embraces humanity's multi-dimensional connection to reality.

Conventional education, born under the umbrella of industrialism and the Newtonian world view, operates out of the closed systemic framework. Conscious and holistic education operate in an open system where all matter, life and energy is interconnected in countless and profound ways.

According to Clark (1981), the systemic world view recognizes the holistic nature of life on the planet. Implicit are the values of interdependence, diversity, cooperation, equilibrium and limits. Clark goes on to explain that ecosystem education demonstrates how the major components of the Earth's ecosystem act as a functional whole. Herein lies the goal of systemic learning: to bring about higher order functioning by enabling learners to understand systemic relationships, both within and among whole systems.

Conscious education recognizes that learners need to be engaged in the exploration of five fundamental global systems: ecological, economic, political, technological and social. What follows is our view on how ecological systemic learning can be approached.

Ecological Systems

> *The planet on which we live is a sphere of rock, orbiting the sun, bathed in radiant energy and the solar wind. Beneath its crust, it is white hot and molten. Upon its surface, continents float and ocean floors spread. Between its dynamic surface and the vacuum of space above, is the thin, fragile layer that is made of humans, plants, animals, and microorganisms that are interdependent with one another and that depend upon land, oceans, and elements to sustain life... The earth's biosphere is a living system that is continuously rebuilding the biochemical basis of life and thereby permitting life-support structures and food chains to exist and flourish.*

W. Kniep, (1990)

To sound a note for the understanding of ecological systems, *Our Planet, Our Home** was developed by Phil Gang (1988). It is a learning system that enables people to see relationships through the manipulation of pictures and

---

* Published by Zephyr Press, Tucson, Arizona, USA

arrows that depict Earth and human resources. The materials facilitate an understanding of how Earth's systems and cycles can work together in near-perfect harmony. It helps people examine today's ecological difficulties and explore solutions which use the Earth's vast material and intellectual resources.

Our Planet, Our Home (OPOH) is experiential. Emphasis is placed on process, conversation, and exploration as a means of enriching knowledge and understanding. The materials stimulate reflective thinking and were developed with the philosophy that it is more important to listen to a learner's concept of relationships than to "give" someone the correct answers. In this format, questions become more important than answers. The process of inquiry and discovery allows learners to determine for themselves how the different Earth systems work in harmony or disharmony.

Originally designed for working with young people, *Our Planet, Our Home* has also become a unique tool for helping older learners make dramatic shifts in ecological thinking. The OPOH system has been presented to adults and youth groups all over the world — school aged children 6-18 as well as university students, "special" learners, teachers, environmental groups, parents, business leaders and social activists. The process and dialogue around developing different constellations of the photographs is actually more important than any "end" picture the group develops.

In presenting these materials one moves from the known to the unknown. In this context, the nomenclature for all of the picture cards is given to the whole group and then several sub-groups develop their own configuration, providing their own meaning. Here is a typical presentation to 15 people:

We are going to divide into three groups of five people and work with the *Our Planet, Our Home* model. Let me share the story behind each photograph. This photo represents our galaxy and the universe. In this photo card we have the Earth and all its systems. This one is a picture of the sun and represents our source of energy — light and heat. This photo represents all of the water on the surface of the planet, not just the oceans, but all the water. Here we have a picture that represents our atmosphere — the air we breathe. And here is the land, the surface of the Earth and a source for nutrients. Now we have a composite picture of the last four circles. This is the biosphere — that part of our planet where all life exists.

Here are some smaller circles. This one represents all of the plants on the planet, and this one all of the animals. Here we have a photo of one particular group of animals — human beings. Finally, we have series of picture cards that represent some human needs — food, transportation, recreation, communication, protection and love.

Your challenge over the next half hour is to work in groups and develop some meaningful relationships using these arrows and these pictures. You may use all of the pictures and all of the arrows, some of the pictures and some of the arrows — or, you can add more arrows and more pictures of your own. It is up to you. At the end of this 30 minute period

be prepared to make a short presentation to
the rest of us, sharing your process of working together and the results you achieved.

Here is one example of what a group in Utah, USA
developed: They arranged the picture cards of the Earth's
spheres, life forms, and human needs in the shape of a
spiral. Then they made an analogy between the nautilus
shell that continually builds upon itself and the potential of
the Earth's systems to grow and provide life and joy for all.

In a thirty minute increment people are able to look at
their personal value system in relation to the ecology of
mind and spirit. In small groups, participants can be heard
saying words and phrases like: "interconnected," "this
can't be separated," "humans are not supposed to be in the
center," "universal love," "it's all one!"

The OPOH experience allows each group to construct
its own context for understanding ecological systems. Because of the divergence in human thought, the chances of
any two groups creating identical pictorial representations
are infinitely small. As a result of this work, people are able
to understand ecological systems because they have constructed the experience themselves. They also have an
opportunity to experience a multitude of perspectives as
other groups share their context.

The following teacher-facilitated OPOH layout describes the exchange between plants and animals (Figure
6.2, Interdependence). The teacher-facilitator engages the
participants by asking them to describe the processes of
exchange that connect plants and animals. *Plants give ani-
mals/humans food, protection and oxygen. Humans/animals give
plants carbon dioxide. Plants need sunlight, earth and water to
survive. Plants give back water to the atmosphere, and when
plants die they fall back to the earth.* The pattern that is

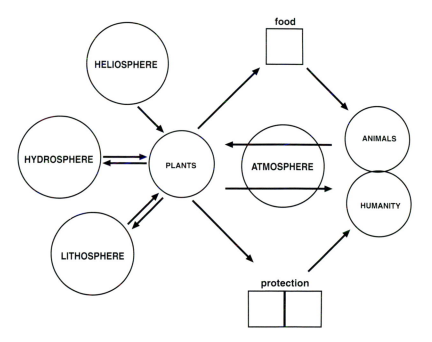

Figure 6.2 Our Planet, Our Home Interdependence

illustrated on page 89 demonstrates that all elements are needed for this system to work. But are they? One by one each picture is removed and the question is raised about its importance. When asked if the system would work without humans, the answer is a resounding *"yes."* What does this mean? For younger children it is enough to facilitate a discussion about personal responsibility to the planet. For older participants this could be a point of philosophical departure to consider the essence of humanity and our purpose.

After working with this system, a nine-year-old child in Sweden exclaimed, *"This is like a family tree of the Earth!"*

TRANSPERSONAL LEARNING

The secret of Education lies in respecting
the pupil. It is not for you to choose
what he shall know, what he shall do.
It is chosen and foreordained, and he
only holds the key to his own secret.

Ralph Waldo Emerson

The prefix, *trans* means "above and beyond, transcending." Thus, transpersonal learning, by definition, embodies learning at all levels. It is learning about the self and one's relationship to life. Through conscious education learners are able to discern their physical, emotional, mental and soul selves.

Transpersonal learning includes the three "i's" of imagination, intuition, and intellect. It implies that body, mind and spirit become one functioning unit in the learning process. This kind of learning goes beyond academics, beyond knowledge, into conscious awareness of life purpose.

Transpersonal learning recognizes that the *whole person* is the learner, and that the bridge to autonomous freedom is built by a process of getting in touch with the inner self. This bridge building is integral to conscious education.

We will now explore the focal points of transpersonal learning, its major objectives and the qualities to be developed in the transpersonal learner.

Focal Points of Transpersonal Learning

Purpose, consciousness and creative thinking form a triangle (Figure 6.3) to deepen one's understanding of the Self. Purpose is aligned with will as the primary energy and takes its position at the top. Consciousness represents love, and creative thinking represents intelligence. These three are the primary attributes for learning. They need to be equally present in the learning environment and are represented by a triangle to honor their stabilizing effect.

PURPOSE

CONSCIOUSNESS   CREATIVE THINKING

Figure 6.3 Focal Points of Transpersonal Learning

Purpose

Purpose gives life meaning. As educators, we may not know the learner's purpose — but the *learner* knows. It is the educator's responsibility to consciously draw forth the innate soul purpose for the learner's recognition.

Consciousness

The consciousness aspect is that which gives meaning to life. Conscious awareness helps learners know that they are connected to all of life.

Creative thinking

Creative thinking nurtures the mind so that learners are empowered to think their own thoughts. It gives them the freedom to explore the world fully through their mind and be creative. The soul resides on the mental plane and provides the impulse for creative thinking.

Creative thinking, consciousness and purpose are all aspects of transpersonal learning. Conscious teaching might focus on these ideas by bringing learners together into a group and discussing a common goal or vision *(Purpose)*. The teacher might ask them to talk about their personal vision — they might draw, sing, act or speak their ideas. In small groups they could share this experience, enabling them to become conscious *(Consciousness)* of the integration of their vision within the group. At this point the role of the teacher is to share pertinent information about the stated common goal or vision. So if the group's goal is to "create a healthy planet" the teacher now shares knowledge as well as where the learners may find additional resources on the current "state of the planet." Thus the learners become informed and can make conscious choices *(Creative thinking)* about their future.

A further understanding lies in the use of a contextual matrix developed by Edward Clark (Figure 6.4, Contextual matrix). In Clark's example the question is posed: *How to live responsibly in a global community?* The matrix can be used by a skilled teacher/facilitator to integrate creative thinking, consciousness and purpose.

Clark contends that the critical element in using the matrix lies in its approach to develop open-ended questions, what he calls questions worth thinking about. There is no right or wrong response, only responses that come from the seat of self-reflective consciousness. No two people respond the same way. Therefore these questions raise opportunities to understand the essence of diversity.

In using the contextual matrix approach, questions are built around individual and life purpose. They call forth the creativity of the learner to reflect on personal experience and integrate learning across the curriculum. The questions are so open-ended that learners of vastly different ages can respond at their own level from their own personal context.

Major Objectives of Transpersonal Learning

The objectives of transpersonal learning are: 1) to accept and know thyself and 2) to become a world citizen.

To accept and know thyself on all levels leads to transformation of self which opens the door to become a citizen of the world. Acceptance and knowledge of self fosters peace within. As one crosses the bridge to autonomous freedom

"What does it mean to live responsibly as a member of the global community?"

CONTEXTUAL QUESTIONS

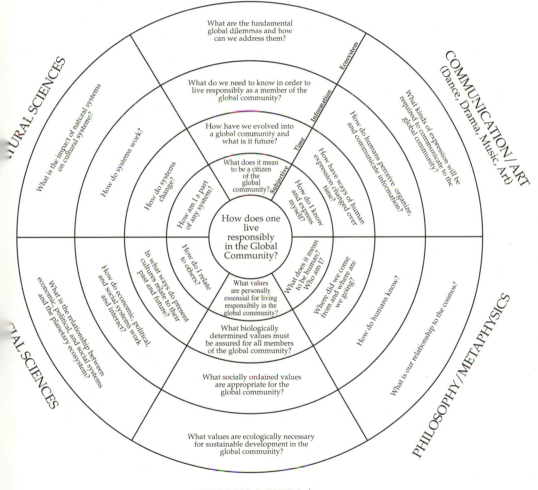

What are the fundamental global dilemmas and how can we address them?

What do we need to know in order to live responsibly as a member of the global community?

How have we evolved into a global community and what is it future?

What does it mean to be a citizen of the global community?

How does one live responsibly in the Global Community?

NATURAL SCIENCES

What is the impact of natural systems on cultural systems?

How do systems work?

How do systems change?

How am I a part of any system?

How do I relate to others?

In what ways do present cultures relate to their past and future?

How do economic and social systems work and interact?

What is the relationship between economic, political, and social systems and the planetary ecosystem?

SOCIAL SCIENCES

Ecosystem

Information

Time

Subjective

How do I know and express myself?

How do humans perceive, organize, and communicate information?

How have ways of human expression changed over time?

What kinds of expression will be required to communicate to the global community?

COMMUNICATION/ART (Dance, Drama, Music, Art)

What does it mean to be human? Who am I?

Where did we come from and where are we going?

How do humans know?

What is our relationship to the cosmos?

PHILOSOPHY/METAPHYSICS

What values are personally essensial for living responsibly in the global community?

What biologically determined values must be assured for all members of the global community?

What socially ordained values are appropriate for the global community?

What values are ecologically necessary for sustainable development in the global community?

VALUES/NEEDS

© 1990, Edward T. Clark, Jr.

Figure 6.4   A Contextual Matrix

this peace expands from self, to self in relation to others, to self in relation to community, world and universe.

World citizenship, based on shared responsibility, intimates a recognition and acceptance that we are all citizens of one world, equally responsible for the health of the Earth.

Qualities to be Developed by the Transpersonal Learner

>
> Creative independent thinking
> Service orientation
> Cooperation
> Observation
> Communication
> Inner knowing

Creative independent thinking is the ability of learners to think for themselves, to consciously contribute to and participate in life. For children to design their future, they must be able to think reflectively.

Service has its origins in the development of community in which the common good is emphasized.

Cooperation is based on a sense of sharing.

Observation must be modeled by the teacher/facilitator. The modeling process helps learners to develop this skill, and creates the space for observation to be learned naturally. In *Fiery World Volume I* (1969) this quality is explained as follows:

> The quality of observation is one of the principal fiery qualities, but it is not attained easily. It is acquired as slowly as is consciousness......consciousness is strengthened by life itself; observation is strengthened

likewise.... Hence, by all means, training in observation should be introduced in schools, even for small children. An hour devoted to observation is a true lesson in life, and for the teacher this hour will be a lesson in resourcefulness. Begin the refinement of observation upon everyday objects. It would be a mistake to direct the pupils too rapidly to higher concepts. If, for a beginning, the pupil is capable of observing the habitual contents of a room, this will already be an achievement. This is not so easy as it seems to an unobservant eye. Later, by a series of experiments we can accelerate the ability to form impressions. We can propose that the pupil pass through an unfamiliar room at a run and yet with concentrated observation. Thus, it is possible to reveal blindness and assert true keenness of vision. It is necessary to outline a program of tests for all the senses...children are very fond of such tasks. Such exercise of consciousness carry one into the higher spheres.

Communication, both inner and outer—listening, speaking and sharing — is a necessity for all participants in the learning environment.

Inner knowing is achieved by helping the learner to go within and discover true identity. Some ways to encourage this are through questions, meditation and guided imagery.

In the simplest of language, transpersonal learning enables learners to access their true selves.

Chapter Seven

CONSCIOUS EDUCATION
and HOLISM

We want schools that will enable students to encounter, to build relationship and to cooperate with the world. They can only accomplish this with a redirection of energy from a reductionist to a more holistic perspective; that is from one that emphasizes facts and objectivity (I-it) to one that explores interdependency and unity (I-Thou).

Phil Gang (1989)

Conscious education is inspired by the holistic education movement and is celebrated through the window of holism. This reemerging paradigm is based not only on the scientific discoveries of our time, but also on the deep sense of knowing passed down through the ages by our mystical ancestors from east and west, north and south. Conscious education is in Wilber's realm of the transpersonal, and reflects Bailey's soul-infused personality on the bridge to freedom. For conscious education the focus is on raising and transforming consciousness.

THE MOVEMENT TOWARDS HOLISM
IN EDUCATION

The holistic education movement began to crystallize in 1989 when eight concerned educators came together to explore their common vision. Each person represented a particular perspective and was willing to step beyond personal agendas to merge with others in alliance for holistic education.   An agreement was made to listen to differences, support individuality, hold as a common vision the building of a global movement for holistic education, and model a process that no longer uses hierarchical structures but adheres to the process of lateral empowerment.

The original group acknowledged the central theme as spirituality in education and saw themselves as models attempting to develop a process that would empower others along a path of co-creation. Holism was created in mind and heart by speaking openly and working through areas of apparent impasse by "letting go" of the right/wrong dialectic.

To further the process, a conference was designed and each person accepted responsibility for inviting educational change agents. Encouraging diversity, people were invited from different perspectives, to an event called, "Creating a Common Vision for Holistic Education." The information flowed beyond the original invitees and a rush of interest was expressed from many corners of the world.

Eighty-three individuals attended that first conference, held outside of Chicago, USA. As teachers and learners creating a new force in education, we jointly developed the Chicago Statement on Education (see p. 116). With the support from the participants and leadership from the initiators, a decision was made to continue our group effort.

GLOBAL ALLIANCE FOR TRANSFORMING EDUCATION

A steering committee of twelve formed to respond to the ongoing momentum. The group became known as the Global Alliance for Transforming Education (GATE). We were determined to be inclusive and maintain a process of mutuality and equality. We needed to create a process for decision-making yet were reluctant to have one person in charge. Instead we created an executive triangle. We understood the limitations of old managerial systems based on one person at the "top." Two people can create power struggles but three people invite diversity and discussion. It was agreed that the triangle would decide on "daily operating activities" and that all large decisions would return to the group of twelve.

There is no *right* or *wrong* in our process ...just ideas circulating until we reach consensus. We see the vision expanding as more people and new energy join the movement. We give the following words to our mission:

> *To proclaim and promote*
> *a vision of education*
> *that fosters*
> *personal greatness,*
> *social justice,*
> *peace, and*
> *a sustainable environment.*

The vision is not intended to be static, but ever-evolving and organic. GATE members are recognized for their particular contribution and encouraged to be active. GATE understands that dissension and discussion are healthy indicators and encourages individuals to quiet their personal insecurities. This process continues. In the largest context of educational reform we share a common vision. Our ways and means to achieve that vision vary significantly. Beneath all the words, GATE carries a commitment for an education that helps learners connect to the world and realize their potential.

The second annual conference was planned using a similar process. It was held in Colorado (June, 1991) and called, "Expanding the Common Vision." We met and went to a new level of growth. Today the movement is extending itself. Participants are carrying their personal concerns and creating activities which reflect their areas of interest and expertise. And yet they are uniting with GATE to be considered part of a movement for the transformation of education. There are 19 regional coordinators world-wide including, Brazil, Canada, Czechoslovakia, Japan, New Zealand, Sweden, Switzerland and the United States. The Steering Committee continues its innovative work in-group and with others.

In 1991 GATE received a private grant to expand its activities. With the influx of funding it was necessary to re-examine our leadership process. Until this time everything had been accomplished on a volunteer basis. Our goal was to hire an executive director while maintaining our model of non-hierarchical leadership. We created six standing management triangles which included, Regional Support - North America, International Regional Support, Program Development, Financial Administration and Policies, Marketing and Networking and Multicultural Outreach.

An outgrowth of this last conference is the publication of the document: ***EDUCATION 2000: A Holistic Perspective.*** Part One of this publication, the vision statement, concludes this chapter.

EDUCATION 2000
A Holistic Perspective

I. The Vision Statement
Including the Chicago Statement on Education

Preamble

We are educators, parents, and citizens from diverse backgrounds and educational movements who share a common concern for the future of humanity and all life on Earth.

We believe that the serious problems affecting modern educational systems reflect a deeper crisis in our culture: the inability of the predominant industrial/technological worldview to address, in a humane and life-affirming manner, the social and planetary challenges that we face today.

We believe that our dominant cultural values and practices, including emphasis on competition over cooperation, consumption over sustainable resource use, and bureaucracy over authentic human interaction have been destructive to the health of the ecosystem and to optimal human development as well.

As we examine this culture-in-crisis. we also see that our systems of education are anachronistic and dysfunctional. In sharp contrast to the conventional use of the word *education,* we believe that our culture must restore the original meaning of the word, "to draw forth." In this context, *education* means caring enough to draw forth the greatness that is within each unique person.

The purpose of this Statement is to proclaim an alternative vision of education — one which is a life-affirming and democratic response to the challenges of the l990s and beyond. Because we value diversity and encourage a wide variety of methods, applications, and practices, it is a vision toward which educators may strive in their various ways. There is not complete unanimity, even among those of us who endorse this document, on all of the statements presented here. The vision transcends our differences and points us in a direction that offers a humane resolution to the crisis of modern education.

Principle I. Educating for Human Development

We assert that the primary—indeed the fundamental—purpose of education is to nourish the inherent possibilities of human development. Schools must be places that facilitate the learning and whole development of all learners. Learning must involve the enrichment and deepening of relationships to self, to family and community members, to the global community, to the planet, and to the cosmos. These ideas have been expressed eloquently and put into practice by great educational pioneers such as Pestalozzi, Froebel, Dewey, Montessori, Steiner, and many others.

Unfortunately, public education has never had optimal human development as its primary purpose. Historical literature makes it clear that school systems were organized to increase national productivity by inculcating habits of obedience, loyalty, and discipline. The "restructuring" and "excellence" literature of the 1980s and l990s continues to be permeated with a concern for the productivity and competitiveness of the national economy, and seeks to harness the abilities and dreams of the next generation to the goal of economic development. We believe that human development must be served before economic development.

We call for a renewed recognition of human values which have been eroded in modern culture—harmony, peace, cooperation, community, honesty, justice, equality, compassion, understanding, and love. The human being is more complex, more whole, than his or her roles as worker or citizen. If a nation—through its schools, its child welfare policies, and its competitiveness—fails to nurture self-understanding, emotional health, and democratic values, then ultimately economic success will be undermined by a moral collapse of society. Indeed, this is happening already. as is made clear by the drug epidemic and the pressing problems of crime, alcoholism, child abuse, political and corporate corruption, teen alienation and suicide, and violence in the schools. We must nurture healthy human beings in order to have a healthy society and a healthy economy. The economic system surely requires a skilled, dependable work force. We can best secure this work force by treating young people as human beings first and future workers secondarily. Only people who live full, healthy, meaningful lives can be truly productive. We call for a greater balance between the needs of economic life and these human ideals which transcend economics and which are necessary for responsible action.

Principle II. Honoring Students as Individuals

We call for each learner—young and old—to be recognized as unique and valuable. This means welcoming personal differences and fostering in each student a sense of tolerance, respect, and appreciation for human diversity. Each individual is inherently creative, has unique physical, emotional, intellectual, and spiritual needs and abilities, and possesses an unlimited capacity to learn.

We call for a thorough rethinking of grading, assessment, and standardized examinations. We believe that the primary function of evaluation is to provide feedback to the student and teacher in order to facilitate the learning process. We suggest that "objective" scores do not truly serve the learning or optimal development of students. We have been so busy measuring the measurables that we have neglected those aspects of human development which are immeasurably more important. Besides neglecting important dimensions of all learners, standardized tests also serve to eliminate those who cannot be standardized. In successful innovative schools around the world, grades and standardized tests have been replaced by personalized assessments which enable students to become inner directed. The natural result of this practice is the development of self-knowledge, self-discipline, and genuine enthusiasm for learning.

We call for an expanded application of the tremendous knowledge we now have about learning styles, multiple intelligences, and the psychological bases of learning. There is no longer any excuse to impose learning tasks, methods, and materials *en masse* when we know that any group of students will need to learn in different ways, through different strategies and activities. The work being done on multiple intelligences demonstrates that an area of strength such as bodily kinesthetic, musical, or visual spatial can be tapped to strengthen areas of weakness such as linguistic or logical-mathematical.

We question the value of educational categories such as "gifted," "learning disabled," and "at-risk." Students of all ages differ greatly across a full spectrum of abilities, talents, inclinations, and backgrounds. Assigning these labels does not describe a learner's personal potentials, it simply defines one in relation to the arbitrary expectations of the system. The term "at-risk" is especially pernicious: It serves to uphold the competitive, homogeneous goals of the educational system by ignoring the personal experiences and perceptions which lie behind a particular student's difficulties. We suggest, instead, that schooling should be transformed so as to respect the individuality of every person—that we can build a true learning community in which people learn from each other's differences, are taught to value their own personal strengths, and are empowered to help one another. As a result, each learner's individual needs will be met.

Principle III. The Central Role of Experience

We affirm what the most perceptive educators have argued for centuries: education is a matter of experience. Learning is an active, multisensory engagement between an individual and the world, a mutual contact which empowers the learner and reveals the rich meaningfulness of the world. Experience is dynamic and ever growing. The goal of education must be to nurture natural, healthy growth through experience, and not to present a limited, fragmented, predigested "curriculum" as the path to knowledge and wisdom.

We believe that education should link the learner to the wonders of the natural world through experiential approaches that immerse the student in life and nature. Education should connect the learner to the workings of the social world through real-life contact with the economic and social life of the community. And education should acquaint the learner with the realm of his or her own inner world through the arts, honest dialogue, and times of quiet reflection—for without this knowledge of the inner self, all outward knowledge is shallow and without purpose.

Principle IV. Holistic education

We call for wholeness in the educational process, and for the transformation of educational institutions and policies required to attain this aim. Wholeness implies that each academic discipline provides merely a different perspective on the rich, complex, integrated phenomenon of life. Holistic education celebrates and makes constructive use of evolving, alternate views of reality and multiple ways of knowing. It is not only the intellectual and vocational aspects of human development that need guidance and nurturance, but also the physical, social, moral, aesthetic, creative, and—in a nonsectarian sense—spiritual aspects. Holistic education takes into account the numinous mystery of life and the universe in addition to the experiential reality.

Holism is a reemerging paradigm, based on a rich heritage from many scholarly fields. Holism affirms the inherent interdependence of evolving theory, research, and practice. Holism is rooted in the assumption that the universe is an integrated whole in which everything is connected. This assumption of wholeness and unity is in direct opposition to the paradigm of separation and fragmentation that prevails in the contemporary world. Holism corrects the imbalance of reductionist approaches through its emphasis on an expanded conception of science and human possibility. Holism carries significant implications for human and planetary ecology and evolution. These implications are discussed throughout this document.

Principle V. New Role of Educators

We call for a new understanding of the role of the teacher. We believe that teaching is essentially a vocation or calling, requiring a blend of artistic sensitivity and scientifically grounded practice. Many of today's educators have become caught in the trappings of competitive professionalism: tightly controlled credentials and certification, jargon and special techniques, and a professional aloofness from the spiritual, moral and emotional issues inevitably involved in the process of human growth. We hold, rather, that educators ought to be facilitators of learning, which is an organic, natural process and not a product that can be turned out on demand. Teachers require the autonomy to design and implement learning environments that are appropriate to the needs of their particular students.

We call for new models of teacher education which include the cultivation of the educator's own inner growth and creative awakening. When educators are open to their own inner being, they invite a co-learning, co-creating process with the learner. What teaching requires is an exquisite sensitivity to the challenges of human development, not a prepackaged kit of methods and materials. We call for learner-centered educators who display a reverence and a respect for the individual. Educators should be aware of and attentive to each learner's needs, differences, and abilities and be able to respond to those needs on all levels.

Educators must always consider each individual in the contexts of family, school, society, the global community, and the cosmos.

We call for the debureaucratization of school systems, so that schools (as well as homes, parks, the natural world, the workplace, and all places of learning) can be places of genuine human encounter. Today's restructuring literature emphasizes "accountability," placing the teacher at the service of administrators and policy makers. We hold instead that the educator is accountable, above all, to the young people who seek a meaningful understanding of the world they will someday inherit.

Principle VI. Freedom of Choice

We call for meaningful opportunities for real choice at every stage of the learning process. Genuine education can only take place in an atmosphere of freedom. Freedom of inquiry, of expression, and of personal growth are all required. In general, students should be allowed authentic choices in their learning. They should have a significant voice in determining curriculum and disciplinary procedures, according to their ability to assume such responsibility. However, we recognize that some instructional approaches will remain largely adult-guided due to philosophical convictions or because they serve special student populations. The point is that families and students need to be free to choose such approaches, and free not to.

Families should have access to a diverse range of educational options in the public school systems. In place of the current system which offers a handful of "alternatives," public education should be comprised of numerous alternatives. It must no longer be the mission of public education to impose a homogenized culture on a diverse society. There is still a need for non-public schools, which tend to be more receptive to far-reaching innovations, and which are more capable of embodying the values of particular religious or other closely knit communities. Families should have freedom to educate their children at home, without undue interference from public authorities. Home schooling has proven to be educationally, socially, and morally nourishing for many children and families.

Principle VII. Educating for a Participatory Democracy

We call for a truly democratic model of education to empower all citizens to participate in meaningful ways in the life of the community and the planet. The building of a truly democratic society means far more than allowing people to vote for their leaders—it means empowering individuals to take an active part in the affairs of their community. A truly democratic society is more than the "rule of the majority"—it is a community in which disparate voices are heard and genuine human concerns are addressed. It is a society open to constructive change when social or cultural change is required.

In order to maintain such a community, a society must be grounded in a spirit of empathy on the part of its citizens—a willingness to understand and experience compassion for the needs of others. There must be a recognition of the common human needs which bind people together into neighborhoods, nations, and the planetary community. Out of this recognition there must be a concern for justice. In order to secure these high ideals, citizens must be enabled to think critically and independently. True democracy depends on a populace able to discern truth from propaganda, common interests from partisan slogans. In an age when politics are conducted via "sound bytes" and deceptive public relations, critical inquiry is more vital than ever to the survival of democracy.

These are all educational tasks. Yet the teaching/ learning process cannot foster these values unless it embodies them. The learning environment must itself revolve around empathy, shared human needs, justice, and the encouragement of original, critical thinking. Indeed, this is the essence of true education; it is the Socratic ideal, which has rarely been realized in educational systems.

Principle VIII. Educating for Global Citizenship

We believe that each of us—whether we realize it or not—is a global citizen. Human experience is vastly wider than any single culture's values or ways of thinking. In the emerging global community, we are being brought into contact with diverse cultures and worldviews as never before in history. We believe that it is time for education to nurture an appreciation for the magnificent diversity of human experience and for the lost or still uncharted potentials within human beings. Education in a global age needs to address what is most fully, most universally human in the young generation of all cultures.

Global education is based on an ecological approach, which emphasizes the connectedness and interdependence of nature and human life and culture. Global education facilitates the awareness of an individual's role in the global ecology, which includes the human family and all other systems of the earth and universe. A goal of global education is to open minds. This is accomplished through interdisciplinary studies, experiences which foster understanding, reflection and critical thinking, and creative response. Global education reminds us that all education and all human activity need to rest on principles which govern successful ecological systems. These principles include the usefulness of diversity, the value of cooperation and balance, the needs and rights of participants, and the need for sustainability within the system.

Other important components of global education include understanding causes of conflict and experiencing the methods of conflict resolution. At the same time, exploring social issues such as human rights, justice, population pressures, and development is essential to an accurate understanding of the causes of war and conditions for peace.

Since the world's religions and spiritual traditions have such enormous impact, global education encourages understanding and appreciation of them and of the universal values they proclaim, including the search for meaning, love, compassion, wisdom, truth, and harmony. Thus, education in a global age addresses what is most fully and universally human.

Principle IX. Educating for Earth Literacy

We believe that education must spring organically from a profound reverence for life in all its forms. We must rekindle a relationship between the human and the natural world that is nurturing, not exploitive. This is at the very core of our vision for the twenty-first century. The planet Earth is a vastly complex, but fundamentally unitary living system, an oasis of life in the dark void of space. Post-Newtonian science, systems theory, and other recent advances in modern thought have recognized what some ancient spiritual and mythological traditions have taught for centuries: The planet, and all life upon it, form an interdependent whole. Economic, social, and political institutions must engender a deep respect for this interdependence. All must recognize the imperative need for global cooperation and ecological sensitivity, if humankind is to survive on this planet. Our children require a healthy planet on which to live and learn and grow. They need pure air and water and sunlight and fruitful soil and all the other living forms that comprise Earth's ecosystem. A sick planet does not support healthy children.

We call for education that promotes earth literacy to include an awareness of planetary interdependence, the congruence of personal and global well-being, and the individual's role and scope of responsibility. Education needs to be rooted in a global and ecological perspective, in order to cultivate in younger generations an appreciation for the profound interconnectedness of all life. Earth education involves a holistic assessment of our planet and the processes that sustain all life. Central to this study are knowledge of basic support systems for life, energy flows, cycles, interrelationships, and change. Earth education is an integrative field including politics, economics, culture, history, and personal and societal change processes.

Principle X. Spirituality and Education

We believe that all people are spiritual beings in human form who express their individuality through their talents, abilities, intuition, and intelligence. Just as the individual develops physically, emotionally, and intellectually, each person also develops spiritually. Spiritual experience and development manifest as a deep connection to self and others, a sense of meaning and purpose in daily life, an experience of the wholeness and interdependence of life, a respite from the frenetic activity, pressure and over-stimulation of contemporary life, the fullness of creative experience, and a profound respect for the numinous mystery of life. The most important, most valuable part of the person is his or her inner, subjective life—the self or the soul.

The absence of the spiritual dimension is a crucial factor in self-destructive behavior. Drug and alcohol abuse, empty sexuality, crime and family breakdown all spring from a misguided search for connection, mystery, and meaning and an escape from the pain of not having a genuine source of fulfillment.

We believe that education must nourish the healthy growth of the spiritual life, not do violence to it through constant evaluation and competition. One of the functions of education is to help individuals become aware of the connectedness of all life. Fundamental to this awareness of wholeness and connectedness is the ethic expressed in all of the world's great traditions: *"What I do to others I do to myself."* Equally fundamental to the concept of connectedness is the empowerment of the individual. If everyone is connected to everyone and everything else, then the individual can and does make a difference.

By fostering a deep sense of connection to others and to the Earth in all its dimensions, holistic education encourages a sense of responsibility to self, to others, and to the planet. We believe that this responsibility is not a burden, but rather arises out of a sense of connection and empowerment. Individual, group, and global responsibility is developed by fostering the compassion that causes individuals to want to alleviate the suffering of others, by instilling the conviction that change is possible and by offering the tools to make those changes possible.

Conclusion[*]

As we approach the twenty-first century, many of our institutions and professions are entering a period of profound change. We in education are beginning to recognize that the structure, purposes, and methods of our profession were designed for an historical period which is now coming to a close. The time has come to transform education so as to address the human and environmental challenges which confront us.

We believe that education for this new era must be holistic. The holistic perspective is the recognition that all life on this planet is interconnected in countless profound and subtle ways. The view of Earth suspended alone in the black void of space underscores the importance of a global perspective in dealing with social and educational realities. Education must nurture respect for the global community of humankind.

Holism emphasizes the challenge of creating a sustainable, just, and peaceful society in harmony with the Earth and its life. It involves an ecological sensitivity —a deep respect for both indigenous and modern cultures as well as the diversity of life forms on the planet. Holism seeks to expand the way we look at ourselves and our relationship to the world by celebrating our innate human potentials— the intuitive, emotional, physical, imaginative, and creative, as well as the rational, logical, and verbal.

Holistic education recognizes that human beings seek meaning, not just fact or skills, as an intrinsic aspect of their full and healthy development. We believe that only healthy, fulfilled human beings create a healthy society. Holistic education nurtures the highest aspirations of the human spirit.

---

[*] This conclusion is *The Chicago Statement on Education* adopted by eighty international holistic educators at Chicago, Illinois in June 1990.

Holistic education is not one particular curriculum or methodology; it is a set of working assumptions which include the following:

- Education is a dynamic, open human relationship.

- Education cultivates a critical awareness of the many contexts of learners' lives—moral, cultural, ecological, economic, technological, political.

- All persons hold vast multi-faceted potentials which we are only beginning to understand. Human intelligence is expressed through diverse styles and capacities, all of which we need to respect.

- Holistic thinking involves contextual, intuitive, creative, and physical ways of knowing.

- Learning is a lifelong process. All life situations may facilitate learning.

- Learning is both an inner process of self-discovery and a cooperative activity.

- Learning is active, self-motivated, supportive, and encouraging of the human spirit.

- A holistic curriculum is interdisciplinary, integrating both community and global perspectives.

Supporting the GATE Initiative

We invite individuals, groups, associations, and organizations who support this vision statement to join this ever expanding network of transforming agents. GATE is a non-profit membership organization, supported by member fees and donations. If you would like membership information or are interested in creating a dialogue, please write to the Global Alliance for Transforming Education, 4202 Ashwoody Trail, Atlanta, GA 30319 USA. 404/458-5678. FAX 404/454-9749.

PART III
THE TRANSFORMATION PROCESS

Chapter Eight

A BLUEPRINT FOR TRANSFORMING EDUCATION

In June, 1990 the authors brought to the GATE conference a blueprint for transforming education comprised of eight partnership circles rotating around "Educating for the Twenty-First Century."

Through a process of integration and exchange of ideas, this blueprint evolved into the GATE partnership model seen on the following page.

TRANSFORMATIONAL PROCESS

What is transformational process? What does transforming education look like? Where are the people who can mobilize change?

Transformational process expands consciousness. It is the conscious crossing of the bridge toward autonomous freedom. It is creating a space for individuals to experience freedom of thought and action, personal responsibility, interdependence, trust and spirituality — the "ways of being" discussed in Chapter One.

The authors believe that to generate the momentum necessary to take teaching and learning to its next stage — the stage of conscious education — requires a vast network of participating transformers representing a broad spectrum of society. When one thinks about the immensity of this challenge, it might be easy to say, "Impossible!" Yet history indicates that, when the timing is right, change can occur like a bolt of lightning.

GATE PARTNERSHIPS

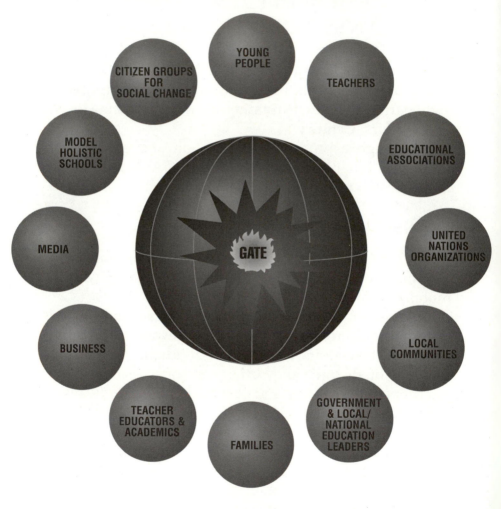

FOR TRANSFORMING EDUCATION

We believe that as the twentieth century comes to a close, our culture is primed for dynamic change. We are reminded too, of the famous words of Margaret Mead:

> Never doubt that a small group of
> committed people can change the world —
> indeed it's the only thing that ever has.

It is our vision that groups of people in local communities all over the world, who are aligned with the ideas of conscious education, will become effective agents of change.

The GATE partnership model is an excellent example of a starting point. Individuals and groups representing the various constituencies are invited to participate in local, national or international meetings. The purpose of these meetings is to help people become catalysts for educational transformation. Our experiences reveal that the components that drive the transformational process, guiding these kinds of meetings include:

1. The use of reflective questioning
2. An opportunity to tell personal stories
3. An understanding of the role of assumptions
4. A description of natural change process
5. Creating the space for personal empowerment
6. Clarifying the vision, leading to creating structures that embody the vision

The process we now describe is an ongoing learning experience. It grows and changes as we discover the nuances in different groups and respond to their issues, needs and focus.

TRANSFORMING EDUCATION:
A CONFERENCE
FOR EDUCATIONAL CHANGE AGENTS

During this four day experience participants have an opportunity to look at the present cultural revolution and its implications for educational transformation. The process begins with people working in small groups discussing the following questions: *What are your images of an ideal school?* and *What do you want people to know?* After a time they share their individual insights with the whole group. We have presented these questions in a wide variety of situations with vastly different groups of people. Invariably, the responses have been in the affective domain — the domain of conscious education.

At this point in the process there is an exploration into cultural change and paradigm shifts in human history, paralleling the ideas presented at the beginning of Chapter Two. This leads into a discussion of "old" (brain antagonistic) and "new" (brain compatible) assumptions, discussed at the end of Chapter Four.

The vision statement, *Education 2000: A Holistic Perspective* is now explored in the context of "new" assumptions. An open discussion concerning the ten principles and their application ensues.

Afterwards, small groups are formed to allow the participants to share their personal stories with each other. They describe their path or journey and their reasons for wanting to transform education. In this dialogue they also talk about the gifts and talents they bring to the transformation process. These small groups finish by generating questions they have about Education 2000 or the transformation process. Here are some examples: How do we deal with resistance to change? How do we better prepare teachers? What are the purposes of schooling? How do we get parents involved? How do you connect out-of-school learning to formal schooling? How do we get different ways of knowing into the classroom? How do we begin to get real global education? How do we develop commonalties among diverse peoples?

Participants now have an opportunity to respond to any one of these questions in small working groups. If they form groups of four, then the whole group explores each of the four questions that are brought forth. Here we discover that people really "know" the answers — from an intuitive level.

To ground the previous experiences, people are given an opportunity to work with *Our Planet, Our Home* as described in Chapter Six. This is a concrete example in transformative learning. By working in groups and by engaging in the language of "connectedness" the participants begin to experience conscious education.

The language of "connectedness" leads into the presentation of the Bridge of Conscious education. Here people begin to experience the soul's journey and the possibility for expanding consciousness. At the end of this experience each person receives a print-out of the seven cosmic laws and principles from Chapter Five. Later on, they will share actual teaching/learning situations in which these principles are applied.

Having explored the processes for conscious learning, we now present conscious education form — the guiding structure for content, as described in Chapter Six.

Then the national award-winning film, *Why Do These Kids Love School* (Fadiman, 1990) is viewed. This film describes learning communities in the United States that have incorporated elements of the new paradigm in education.

The stage has been set for a dialogue around the process of change. The theory that individuals, groups, and organizations all move through five significant phases during transformation is presented. In succession, they are: unaware, aware, understanding, re-creating vision and change. No stage is seen as better than another, just different. By trusting the process and offering support, acceptance and appreciation for others —wherever they are — conscious leaders realize how they can facilitate the transformation process.

The meeting continues with a session devoted to personal vision-building. Participants are asked to "draw" or "artistically design" their vision for education and to place themselves in the picture. Using art supplies, they begin to explore their intuitive and creative potential. These pictures are now shared in small groups.

The final exercise is sparked by two questions: *To transform education, what do you want to see happen in your local community?* and, *What are you willing to do to make this happen?*

Thus, the blueprint for change is not a single imprint, but an ongoing vibration or ripple, imbued with personal meaning and transformational process.

CONCLUSION

There is a road, no simple highway.
Between the dawn and the dark of night.
And if you go, no one may follow,
That path is for your steps alone.

Ripple in still water,
When there is no pebble tossed,
Nor wind to blow.

You who choose to lead must follow.
But if you fall, you fall alone.
If you should stand, then who's to guide you.
If I knew the way I would take you home.

Robert Hunter (Ripple, 1969)

The writers of this book cooperate as a triangle. We visualize and explore the possibilities for an evolving planetary consciousness. We meet in person, talk by telephone, communicate electronically through fax and electronic mail, and are constantly bringing ideas into form. It is our contention that when two or more people agree on a thought or an activity, it is the beginning of creating that reality.

We see ourselves as seeding ideas. We diagram, network, send letters and share the thoughts with colleagues all over the world. We are learning how to create the new and build bridges between the old and the new. We see our process as a reflection of our inner commitments to merge with others for the transformation of consciousness on our planet. We support each other in our growth and trust that we are in service to the world. This is our attempt to create a sense of personal relevance and potency as well as harmony with life.

Our process is to be who we are. This requires inner dialogue. If thoughts are reflective of inner understanding then it is these thoughts that develop identity. Thoughts create momentum. If people say one thing and do another then thoughts are expressed as only empty words. As each of us comes to understand who he or she is, we speak the words that express our identity.

The three of us maintain our search for inner identity and external unity. We model a process that focuses on a common vision. The mutual vision we hold is our commitment to the expansion of consciousness for planetary well-being. Personal issues are addressed in terms of the vision, supporting the cosmic law, the *whole is greater than the sum of the parts*. We encourage each other to stand in our personal truth, in alignment with the vision. We modify our behavior as if we were tuning a violin. We know that our outer life is only a reflection of our inner life. We are each constantly attempting to find answers within. We seek peace while remaining in our personal truth. We are committed to addressing our inner dynamics for releasing personal barriers.

We know that for the accomplishment of world peace there must be room for diversity, and at the same time a bonding must occur. This bonding occurs in an atmosphere of mutual support. It is in listening and accepting that barriers are released. We experience each other in our own personal context.

Modeling the process is knowing "and living" that global consciousness comes from personal peace and self-actualization. In our process, the expansion of consciousness is the merging of mind and heart into one essence. It is the experience of *being* that is more important than any particular product. We explore our interconnectedness and celebrate our differences.

We operate on the principle of right human relations with *harmlessness* as the keynote. This is conscious living, which includes right thought, right speech and right action, reflecting that harmlessness is aligned with the Law of love. Consciously loving one another, we bring out the best in each other, encouraging growth and letting go of limiting beliefs. We appreciate our individuality and we simultaneously have our group mind.

We have discussed our group wholeness through the dynamic interplay of our triangle. Holding the common vision for expanding consciousness through education as our point of focus, gave us the freedom to interact openly, honestly, fearlessly, and with personal integrity. We each became leaders in our own right. We have learned to trust the process.

We are now exploring processes that reflect transpersonal growth through conscious education. We have learned that defining the vision, working in triangles, trusting, and sharing a spiritual perspective are some of the ingredients.

We also know that it requires modeling a process which encourages and invites others to co-join in any activity. In the past, teaching has connoted *power over*... "imparting information to." In conscious education we are suggesting that the teacher is the visionary leader, holding the space in which information is drawn from every learner.

This vision-holder works with others involved in the process to further expand consciousness. For conscious education this means that every individual is a leader. This is also true within the classroom. It means we are ready to take the next step - to embrace conscious leadership.

Profound realizations

trickle through

consciousness

as we dance our

way through

life's rhythm.

Awakened by the

possibilities of being

and attuned to

co-creation

we walk in silence

respecting the moment.

The pulse, the vibration,

the flow,

are channels

we seek for

greater knowing

and personal reflection.

REFERENCES

Arms, M. and Denman, D. *Touching the World,* (New York: Charles Scribner's Sons, 1975)

Assagioli, R. *Psychosynthesis Typology* ...Psychosynthesis Monographs (London, England: Institute of Psychosynthesis, 1983)

Bailey, A.A., *Education in the New Age*, (New York: Lucis Publishing Co., 1954)

Bailey, A.A., *Esoteric Psychology Volumes I & II.* (New York: Lucis Publishing Co., 1962)

Bailey. A.A., *A Treatise on Cosmic Fire,* (New York: Lucis Publishing Co., 1925)

Berry, T., *The Ecozoic Period,* Unpublished manuscript, March, 1990.

Berry, T., *The Dream of the Earth,* (San Francisco: Sierra Club Books, 1988)

Blavatsky, H.P., *The Secret Doctrine*, (Pasadena, CA: Theosophical University Press, 1988, originally published in 1888)

Capra, F., *The Turning Point*, (New York: Simon and Schuster, 1982)

Carin, A., and Sund, R., *Developing Questioning Techniques: A Self Concept Approach,* (Columbus, OH: Charles Merrill Publishing, 1971)

Chopra, D., *Quantum Healing*, (New York: Bantam Books, 1989)

Clark, E. T., "America 2000: A Holistic Perspective," Unpublished Paper, 1992.

Clark, E. T. and Coletta, W., *Quest for a Sustainable Society,* (New York: Pergamon Press, 1981)

Coopersmith, S., *The Antecedent of Self Esteem*, (San Francisco: W.H. Freeman, 1967)

Dewey, J., *Experience and Education*, (New York: Collier Books, 1963 originally published in 1938)

Dossey, L., *Space, Time and Medicine*, (New York: Random House, 1982)

Duska, R., and Whelan, M., *Moral development*, (New York: Paulist Press, 1975) p. 46.

Eisler, Riane, *The Chalice and the Blade*, (San Francisco: Harper and Row, 1987)

Fadamin, D., *Why Do These Kids Love School*, (Menlo Park, CA: Concentric Media, 1990)

Fiery World Volume I, paragraph 69, (Agni Yoga Society, 319 W. 107 Street, New York City, 1969)

Fuller, B., *No More Secondhand God*, (Cabondale, IL: Southern Illinois University Press, 1963)

Gang, P. S., *Rethinking Education*, (Atlanta: Dagaz Press, 1989)

Gerber, R., *Vibrational Medicine*, (Santa Fe: Bear & Company, 1988)

Granville, K., *Mind in Motion*, (Newport News, VA: Catalyst Press, 1990)

Harman, W., *Global Mind Change*, (San Francisco: Knowledge Systems, 1988)

Kniep, W., *Next Steps in Global education*, (New York: American Forum for Global education, 1990)

Kohlberg, L., "Moral Education in the School," *School Review*, 1966, 74. 1-30.

Kolb, D., *Experiential learning*, (Englewood Cliffs, NJ: Prentice Hall, 1984)

Krishnamurti, J., *Education and the Significance of Life*, (San Francisco: Harper & Row, 1981, originally published in 1953)

Leakey, R., and Lewin, R., *People of the Lake*, (New York: Anchor Press, 1978)

Lovelock, J., *The Ages of Gaia*, (New York: W.W. Norton & Company, 1988)

McWaters, B., *Conscious Evolution*, (San Francisco: Evolutionary Press, 1982)

Miller, B. A., *The Multigrade Classroom: A Resource Book for Small, Rural Schools*, (Cambridge, MA: Brookline Books, 1989)

Montessori, Maria, *The Erdkinder and the Function of the University*, (Amsterdam, Holland, Association Montessori Internationale, 1937)

Montessori, M., *The Formation of Man*, (Madras, India: Kalakshetra Publications, 1972, originally published in 1955)

Montessori, M., "Gandhi and the Child," India News, XXIII:45, February 4, 1985 (from "Mahatma Gandhi: Essays and Reflections on his Work," Oct. 1939, S. Radhakrishnan, Ed.)

Montessori, M. M., *The Human Tendencies and Montessori Education*, (Amsterdam: AMI Publications, 1956)

Muller, R., *New Genesis*, (New York: Doubleday & Co, 1982; Anacortes, WA: World Happiness & Cooperation, 1990)

Pascarella, P., *The New Achievers*, (Free Press, 1984)

Peck, S., *The Road Less Traveled*, (New York: Simon and Schuster, 1978)

Piaget, J., *The Psychology of Intelligence*, (London: Routledge and Kegan Paul, 1950)

Render, G., and Lemire, D., "A Consciousness/Spirituality Domain Based on an Elaboration of Maslow's Hierarchy," *Holistic education Review*, Summer, 1989, p. 31.

Rogers, C., *Freedom to Learn*, (Columbus, OH: Charles Merrill Publishing, 1969)

Russell, P., *The Global Brain*, (Los Angeles: J.P. Thatcher, Inc., 1983)

Saraydarian, H., *Cosmos in Man*, (Arizona: Walsh & Associates, 1973)

Steiner, R., *The Education of the Child*, (Worcester, G.B.: Billing & Sons Ltd., 1965)

Teilhard de Chardin, P., *The Future of Man*, (William Collins: 1982)

Van Oudenhoven, N., "Act Locally; Think Globally: Some Comments of Pro-Social Behaviour," (Paper Presented at UNICEF Development Education Seminar, Moscow, 1982) p. 2.

Whitehead, A. N., *The Aims of Education*, (New York: The Free Press, 1967) p.7; originally published in 1929)

Wilber, K., "The Spectrum of Development," in Wilber, Kenneth, Ed. *Transformations of Consciousness*, (Boston: Shambala, 1986)

Zukav, G., *The Dancing Wu Li Masters*, (New York: Wm. Morrow & Company, 1979)

Zukav, G., *Science and Spirit*, Proceedings of the 3rd International Forum on New Science, Fort Collins, Colorado, USA, September, 1991.

Zukav, G., *The Seat of the Soul*, (New York: Simon and Shuster, 1989)

About the Authors

Philip S. Gang, Ph.D.

Dr. Phil Gang is a philosopher and leading international proponent for holistic approaches in education. He is founder of The Institute for Educational Studies in Atlanta and serves as Executive Director of GATE, the Global Alliance for Transforming Education, — a world-wide network of global/holistic educators. Dr. Gang has extensive experience as an international lecturer, workshop leader and consultant, and has served as teacher and head of a Montessori school which he founded.

Dr. Gang has presented in Andorra, Australia, Brazil, Costa Rica, Czechoslovakia, Finland, France, Italy, Japan, Mexico, New Zealand, Norway, Puerto Rico, Russia, Sweden, Switzerland, and throughout the United States and Canada. He facilitates workshops titled *Transforming Education* and *Global-Ecocentric Paradigm in Education*, which provide participants with the knowledge and experience to take personal responsibility for change.

Phil is the author of *Rethinking Education,* a detailed view of education for the emerging paradigm. He also developed the teaching system titled *Our Planet, Our Home,* which is used throughout the world to help people become ecologically aware and responsible. Dr. Gang's dynamic vision for education is the foundation for all his work, which above all else encourages and empowers the individual to take personal initiative in affecting change.

Nina Meyerhof Lynn, Ed.D.

Dr. Nina Lynn is the founder of Heart's Bend World Children's Center, located on a 110 acre farm in Newfane, Vermont, USA. For more than twenty years, Nina has provided children opportunities to experience community living, explore personal belief systems and discover common purposes. Through her dynamic efforts and visionary ideals, Heart's Bend is well recognized as an international center for children and youth. The center offers summer camp programs, children's summits, exchange programs and acts as a communication hub uniting children around the world.

Heart's Bend serves as headquarters of the Coalition for Children of the Earth, an international network of individuals and groups established to empower the voice of children as an essential element in creating a better world. To this end, programs are designed for children to become informed and valued citizens and to look upon themselves as potential future leaders. Programs focus on the United Nations and are dedicated to the "We the Peoples Initiative."

Dr. Lynn is a founder of GATE, The Global Alliance for Transforming Education, and continues to be an advocate of holistic learning. As a process facilitator, she travels worldwide consulting with groups striving to transform education. Nina also held a position in the public school system in Newfane, Vermont as a Special Education Administrator. Her willingness to bring new ideas to public education and to assist in their implementation resulted in fifteen years of innovative programming and service to her community.

Dorothy J. Maver, Ph.D.

Dr. Dorothy Maver is an education consultant and co-director of the Institute for Visionary Leadership in Minneapolis, Minnesota, USA, and is a founder and former executive director of the Seven Ray Institute and the University of the Seven Rays. She also serves on the steering committee for GATE, The Global Alliance for Transforming Education. As a keynote speaker and workshop facilitator world wide, Dorothy is recognized as an innovative educator in the fields of psychology, philosophy, health and physical education.

As a private practitioner, Dr. Maver has inspired people of all ages to move forward in their learning process. Her pioneering work has been designed to help individuals and groups realize their potential on all levels - physical, emotional, mental and spiritual. She also strives to help youth gain confidence and achieve their learning potential using Transformational Kinesiology and the *Spectrum Profiler,* an instrument she developed for vocational counseling based on a seven ray typology. She has filmed a companion video titled The Seven Rays: Educating with Purpose.

A creative thinker, writer and workshop facilitator, Dr. Maver is also widely recognized for her work in athletics. As "Dr. Dot", she travels extensively presenting clinics to softball players and coaches, and has developed a revolutionary softball hitting technique known as *The Maver Method.*

The authors invite comments and dialog about *Conscious Education.* You may write to the authors at the following address.

Dagaz Press
P.O. Box 80651
Chamblee, Georgia 30366

Index